The Secret Life
Of Your Cells

The Secret Life
Of Your Cells

Robert B. Stone, Ph.D.

1469 Morstein Road
West Chester, Pennsylvania 19380 USA

The Secret Life of Your Cells
by Robert B. Stone, Ph. D.

Library of Congress Card Number: 89-50767
International Standard Book Number: 0-914918-96-6

Manufactured in the United States of America

Published by Whitford Press,
A division of
Schiffer Publishing, Ltd.
1469 Morstein Road
West Chester, Pennsylvania 19380
Please write for a free catalog.
This book may be purchased from the publisher.
Please include $2.00 postage.
Try your bookstore first.

Contents

Foreword

Your plants know what you are thinking. The cells of your body, even when removed and observed at a distance away, know what you are thinking. The cells of your brain, with which you think, know more than you think they do. And if other primary perception phenomena that have been studied under laboratory conditions for twenty years prove out, the world may never be the same.

When it became fashionable for people to openly talk to their plants in the late 60s and early 70s a man named Cleve Backster made it possible. But it has been only in the past few years that this primary perception has been measured at the cell level in ways that promise to open up new vistas in health care and to provide new substantiation not only for the mind-body connection, but a mind-to-mind connection.

What made Cleve Backster decide to hook up a lie detector to a house plant more than twenty years ago, we may never know. But what has happened since then has far eclipsed the importance of his name being used on a standard polygraph scale or his reputation as a foremost polygraph authority. It has provided insight into a connecting intelligence between all living creatures.

It has pointed to the existence of a primary perception--the knowing of even our most secret thoughts--at even a unicellular level.

The intent of the author is to ring the bells of glad tidings that new approaches to human problems may become available, especially health problems.

What are the effects on human relationships? On diplomacy? On science? I leave that to specialists in these fields. But what I present conclusively on the pages ahead, cannot be wished away, by you, by me or by them. Our thoughts are known. They are known by the cells of our body and probably by other cells at a distance. Cells have a secret life. Part of that secret life is: We can keep no secrets from them. So we may as well harness their power to make a better life for ourselves. This book tells why and how.

Robert B. Stone, Ph.D.
Kaneohe, Hawaii
January 1, 1989

Chapter I

The Solid Evidence
That Cells Communicate
At A Distance

On February 10, 1986, twenty men and women from different states and from Washington D.C. arrived at the laboratory of the Backster Research Foundation in San Diego, California. They came to investigate a phenomenon that would have some scientists totally perplexed, others totally incredulous.

Of the twenty, sixteen were staff and members of the Committee on Techniques for the Enhancement of Human Performance of the National Research Council's Commission on Behavioral and Social Sciences and Education. The specific purpose of the visit was to collect evidence that cells can communicate over a distance.

Simple cells communicate? There was nothing within the parameters of the science we know that could make this possible. Yet on that February day in San Diego, the research methodology was demonstrated. They were shown human cells reacting to events that were taking place even after they had been removed and placed at a distance from the host body.

This visit was part of a two year broader research project and was only the first visit by the entire committee to a field research facility. Each were renowned members of the scientific community, having received recognition in more conventional areas of science. How this group collectively reacted to their observations, and to the material provided them, will be best understood after reviewing their final project report. Were the implications of such cellular communication envisioned, especially in the areas of human health, genetics, immunology, the healing process and the mind-brain-body connection? More about that in later chapters.

More definitive answers to such questions may be decades away, but meanwhile divulging the secret life of cells can mean immediate benefits to the reader. Even though we do not fully understand electrical energy, we can still gain its benefits. Even though we do not fully understand this cellular "energy", we can enjoy benefits for health, skills and human relationships just knowing that it exists.

This knowledge was born in New York City some twenty years ago. It was an occasion when Cleve Backster felt like throwing open a window in his Time Square laboratory and shouting to the world, "Plants can read your thoughts!"

DISCOVERING THE SECRET LIFE OF PLANTS

It was a cold February night in 1966. Cleve Backster had been up most of that evening preparing material for teaching the use of the polygraph to students from law enforcement organizations then attending a six week course of instruction at the Backster School of Lie Detection.

Now it was well after midnight. He sat looking at the only greenery in sight in that concrete megalithic urban center--a rubber plant and a dracena, a large leaved tropical plant similar to a miniature palm tree. It was time he watered them. As he thought about the watering process, he wondered how long osmosis took. How much time would be required for the Dracena plant to receive the water in its leaves once the water was placed in the ground around its roots. He had the equipment to determine this: a resistance recording device, namely the Wheatstone bridge. It is the basis of the galvanic skin response part of the polygraph. If he connected it to a leaf he should observe a straight, upward climb on the polygraph reflecting the arrival of the moisture.

After carrying both plants to the sink and giving them a good watering, he returned the dracena to a location near the polygraph and connected the electrodes to the end of one of the long leaves, using some rubber bands. Making sure there was paper in the read-out machine, he then turned on the instrument. As the paper began to move, there was a downward trend instead of an upward trend. And instead of there being a straight line as he expected there was a serrated line. It traced out a series of small spikes and the recording trended downward.

The electrodes of a polygraph, when connected to a human, pick up changes in the skin's electrical properties. These changes occur when a person tells a lie. No matter how calm the person appears to be outwardly, internal bodily changes automatically occur, such as increased body cell electrical activity.

Backster was thinking in terms of how long it would take the water to go from the roots to the leaf where the electrodes were attached so as to obtain a measurable upward trending of the tracing.

Strangely, the tracing continued to trend in the opposite direction from that which he had expected. The tracing moved down instead of up.

Then, what happened about one minute into the recording was to set the stage for further amazement. The tracing showed a change that, were it from a human, would qualify as a reaction indicative of deception to a crime related question just asked.

PLANTS CAN SENSE OUR CREATIVE OR DESTRUCTIVE THOUGHTS

He decided to do a number of things to threaten the well being of the plant. He reached for the cup of hot coffee in front of him and dunked a leaf of the plant in it. Nothing. Not hot enough. He decided to get a match from another room and burn the leaf.

The instant he held that thought in his mind, there was a sudden and prolonged sweep upward of the recording pen. He had not budged. He had not yet reached for a match. Could the plant have read his mind?

He left and returned with the matches. There had been a second surge upward by the pen. He lit a match and touched the leaf. There was a third upward surge but less than before. The next morning when he showed his associate Robert Henson what had happened, his associate decided to burn the plant. At that instant, a similar reaction occurred. But Backster refused to let him actually harm the plant. When either of them only pretended to harm the plant there was no further reaction.Did the plants know their thoughts so sensitively as to differentiate between when they meant it and when they didn't?

Recalls Backster, "Have you ever been alone in a room but had a feeling of a presence with you? I saw that plant now not as a mass of chemicals, chlorophyll and water, but as something more--a living thing with the capability of some primary type of perception."

The rest of the story is legend. Perhaps you were one of millions who read about this research in *The Secret Life of Plants* by Peter Tompkins and Christopher Bird[1]. Or perhaps you read about it even before in *National Wild Life*, February 1969, or in the scores of media stories and interviews that grew out of that. In March of that year, *Medical World News* commented that at last research in ESP might be on the verge of achieving scientific respectability.

HOW A NEW DIRECTION IN SCIENTIFIC RE-SEARCH WAS TRIGGERED

As a result of a short article in the April 1969 issue of Electro Technology over five thousand scientists bombarded Backster with requests for reprints of the original laboratory research. More than a score of universities indicated they were taking up the research as soon as they could get the desired equipment.

As discourse both written and verbal began to take place between these scientists, many of whom were not able to replicate his results, the term "Backster Effect" began to be used by them, usually in the facetious way, but in accordance with scientific practice of tagging a "discovery" with somebody's name until the explanation or verification can be worked out.The initial research was well-covered in *The Secret Life of Plants*. A research chemist demonstrated he could determine a person's thoughts through a plant.

An electronic technician used a philodendron and claimed to have started his car over two miles away, activated by a thought impulse.

A chemist allegedly recorded an excited reaction in his house plants when he made love to his girl friend eighty miles away.

So much has happened since then. Yes, it appears that plants can "know" our thoughts. Some plants better than others. Some thoughts better than others. But, the simplest living cells appear to read our thoughts too.

Our thoughts or emotions can possibly be known by our liver cells, our heart cells, our kidney cells. Take our mouth cells. Even when removed a distance from our body and monitored with electronic devices, they have been found in more recent research to react measurably to our thoughts or emotions.There is strong evidence that points to our thoughts being known by cells, organisms, plants, animals and brain cells in other people. There is evidence, too, that plants and animals know each other's thoughts.

CAN BRAIN CELLS COMMUNICATE WITH BLOOD CELLS?

Today's prevalence of allopathic approaches to therapy have been given pause. Here is one example why.

A man relaxes, imagines he is inside his circulation system talking to his white blood cells.

"Attention!" he imagines he says to them and he "sees" them respond immediately by coming to a halt. "We need to attack and expel the dead and dying cancer cells. Everybody get to work!"

He sees the white blood cells doing this job and getting rid of the cancer cells weakened by radiation. A remission of the cancer is recorded.

Physicians have already seen what the mind can do when the placebo (actually a sugar pill) is administered. The patient's brain cells, reflecting the belief that "this is a valuable chemical that will make me well," in some way communicates this to the cells or organs involved and healing takes place.

Now this communication is being harnessed and applied through relaxation and imaging as in the hypothetical cancer case just described. The activity is called psychoneuroimmunology; its respect as a growing branch of research is confirmed by the denotation with initials: PNI.

How does PNI work? A possible answer is being supplied by Backster's work with cells, and the discovery of their secret life: a primary perception that has profound philosophical implications which we blithely call "biocommunications."

THE INSECURITY OF INDIVIDUAL SCIENTISTS

What scientist wants to stick his neck out and state categorically that plants can read our minds? Even the idea of plants communicating with plants which Backster has recorded under laboratory conditions is too "far out" a concept to state publicly.

Take the recent findings by two separate groups of plant biologists, one in New Hampshire and the other in Washington state. They have found that trees under insect attack convey warning signals to their fellow trees which then take defensive measures to protect themselves.

Neither group proposed that warning signals were in the form of pure communication. Both groups called the warning signals a type of airborne chemical yet to be discovered. Airborne? How then could they be carried upwind? They are willing to extend their concept of plants as being more complex and capable of more sophisticated behavior than previously thought possible through chemical behavior. But communication between plants in some telepathic or psychic way? Not yet. Backster is undaunted. Being a scientist himself his efforts with other scientists have been toward having them keep an open mind. They may not be willing to believe in the existence of primary perception at the plant level or cellular level, but until all the data has been reviewed, they should not vote it out. An open mind is the hallmark of a scientist. But not all scientists have the courage to display it.

ONE SCIENTIST WITH COURAGE

Meanwhile, Cleve Backster cannot wait. He wants to see people benefit now from the findings, and possibly even some of the world's problems alleviated.

A quick look at the man.

During World War II, he served in the Western Pacific as a commissioned officer in the U.S. Navy and later as an interrogation instructor in the U.S. Army Counter Intelligence Corps. He accepted a post-war position as interrogation specialist with the Central Intelligence Agency where he instituted their still active polygraph program.

Since 1959 he has been training director for some 125 basic polygraph examiner training courses and more than 50 advanced polygraph conferences and seminars. Each of the ten years since 1976 he was reappointed Chairman of the Research and Instrumentation Committee of the American Polygraph Association. He has testified before a Congressional Committee on two occasions as an expert on these matters.

He has also served as a guest instructor at the Department of Defense Polygraph School, the Canadian Police College Polygraph School and the F.B.I. Academy.

For more than twenty years he has laid his reputation as a polygraph expert on the line by pursuing plant and cell research. Still, the Backster Zone Comparison polygraph technique continues to be used as a world standard. His reputation has not suffered nor has the reputation of any serious scientist who have made the professional decision to investigate.

What energy is at work? Does it fall within our electromagnetic spectrum or outside of it? And just as gravity may be considered to be a universal "handshake" can this type of communication be a life signal that connects all creation?

SOME QUESTIONS RAISED BY PLANT COMMUNICATION

Work with plants reveals that plants register fear, pleasure and relief. They respond to threats to their well-being and to the intentions and feelings of other life forms in the same environment.

This appears to be a primary perception because it has been revealed by all the cells that have been monitored, without regard to biological function. Amoeba, paramecium, cells of fruit or vegetables, mold cultures, scrapings from the human mouth, blood, and spermatozoa all appear to respond to your thoughts and mine.

What is the answer? Is there a life force field in which we live, move and have our being? Is Dr. Rupert Sheldrake's morphogenetic field theory, that we are "plugged in" to some larger intelligence, not only true but more widely applicable than even he surmises?

These are heavy questions. But the answers can be only a few thousand lab hours away, only a small fraction of what has already been invested in, say, cancer research. In fact, it may be one of the factors that will contribute to our understanding of cancer.

Why has this research failed to amass any sizeable volume of hours when it was triggered to begin all over the world in the late 1960s? This deprives us all.

To answer that, let's watch as Backster hooks up a philodendron to a polygraph. He starts the recording device (it is now 2:45

p.m.) and goes for a walk to the store. It is now about six minutes later. He is blocks from the philodendron. Backster has forgotten his wallet. Note that the time is exactly 2:51 plus 20 seconds. He goes back to the lab. Now, let's take a look at the graph. See how smooth it is for the first five minutes. Still no significant philodendron reactions. Wait. Here! Look at this sharp peak on the otherwise smooth line. What time did it take place? At 2:51 plus 20 seconds.

When he made the decision to return, the philodendron knew it. Let's have him do it again. We will repeat this exactly. He will walk for six minutes, then come back. Ready? Set the polygraph again. Away he goes. Now, he is back. Where's the spike on the read-out? There is none.

Why didn't the plant react this time?

The answer to that question is the answer to why researchers throw up their hands, walk away, and report, "The Backster Effect cannot be proved because it is not repeatable."

PLANTS APPEAR TO KNOW
WHEN YOU ARE PLAY-ACTING

Here is apparently why the philodendron did not respond the second time around:

It perceived of the plans in advance.

When the mind knows the protocol of the experiment, the plant apparently perceives that it is just an experiment and not the "real thing." It has no reason to get excited.

Confront classical scientists with the fact that the thing needed to make an experiment scientific, namely protocol, is the very thing that makes it unrepeatable, and they throw their hands up in the air.

Don't blame them. Backster has had to devise ways not only to automate these experiments but to make them spontaneous. Automation fits the concept of protocol. Spontaneity does not. The philodendron registers apprehension when a dog passes by. But take a dog by again to demonstrate this to another scientist. The philodendron registers nothing.

Put live brine shrimp into boiling water and the plants react violently. Repeat it and there is much less of a reaction and perhaps none at all. There are many subtleties involved here but Backster believes that basically the plants get used to the death of the shrimp. They adapt to it. They adjust to their environment.

Accidentally cut your finger and the plants receive signals from the dying cells in the drying blood and there is their reaction in black and white. Do it again purposely and the results are not the same.

The laws of gravity and other physical laws that we seem to understand function both in the laboratory and outside of the laboratory. But once you begin to take biocommunication out of real life and put it into synthetic environments, it does not function as if these environments were real. The need for this communication must be derived from life itself, preferably from the survival of life. Survival is probably what primary perception is all about. Apparently it does not exist to play games.

This poses a serious problem for conventional scientists. They follow a simple protocol that produces results for Backster, but it produces no results for them. They do not accept the one change: it was spontaneous in his case, planned in theirs.

Benefits for parents, children, teachers – all of us – must wait for this hurdle to be crossed by the professionals. Then these benefits will likely materialize quite quickly.

EVEN EXPECTATION AND BELIEF ARE COMMUNICATED TO CELLS AND PLANTS

Furthermore, skeptical scientists are injecting another failure factor into the experiment. Expectation and belief are a catalyst to mind research. A green light. Skepticism is a block to mind research. A red light. An example of this took place in the Soviet Union with research in psychokinesis, moving objects without touching them. The subject did this readily on a daily basis with friendly colleagues under strict laboratory conditions. But when skeptical scientists were present to observe, it often took twice as long. The subject had to work against not only standard inertia and friction factors but also the newly added mental opposition factors interposed by the visiting skeptics.

Psychic research has been plagued with this factor. Most psychics no longer agree to demonstrate their ability to skeptical observers. Naturally, this contributes to the skepticism of those so refused. It is a Catch-22 situation for the psychic. If the psychic agrees to demonstrate in a hostile field of consciousness, failure is likely and skepticism reinforced anyhow.

Is humanity being forced to take sides? Either you believe the ability of brain neurons, plants, and single cell organisms to transcend space in their cognizant ability, or you don't. The non-believers had better stay out of our way, because as the pages ahead show, we believers are busy getting a handle on the secret life of our cells as a boon to survival.

Backster hopes this polarization is unnecessary. He feels there is a way for so-called objective scientists to stay in the ball game.

He is studying new ways to "fool" cell organisms and animals by bringing real life into the laboratory. It is important for him and the serious scientists in this field to provide ways for "outside" scientists to fit in. Skepticism has been a wholesome state of mind for scientists in the past. There should be a way to neutralize its laboratory effects.

The Backster Effect, as his results with plants and more simple life forms has come to be less than affectionately known, has divided interested scientists worldwide into two camps in an almost irrevocable way:

Those who have seen it at work cannot have their belief shaken by the non-belief of others. And the non-belief of others will not readily give way to the technical papers of the believers.

Even an act of Congress may not help.

There was such an act in June 1981. The Committee on Science and Technology for the U.S. House of Representatives reported then in its "Survey of Science and Technology Issues Present and Future" that "recent experiments in remote viewing and other studies in parapsychology suggest that there is an 'interconnectedness' of the human mind with other minds and with matter...Experiments in mind-mind interconnectedness have yielded some encouraging results...The implication of these experiments is that the human mind may be able to obtain information independent of geography and time."

There is an organization of people in the United States who believe that the earth is flat. They are ordinary people, sound in body, sound in mind, and well-meaning. Skepticism is here to stay.

We need to continue our work and not delay until some kind of unanimous acceptance has been achieved, so that biocommunications can begin to contribute to the welfare of humankind and make everyday a better day for all.

OUR THOUGHTS ARE KNOWN

The concept of our thoughts being known is intimidating to everyone. "You mean to say that my wife knows when I am thinking of another woman?" Maybe. But perhaps the subconscious brain neurons that are her receptors in this case react with, "So what?" and it never reaches her conscious mind.

"You mean to say my competitor knows what my plans are?"

Maybe. But perhaps the brain neurons that are your competitor's receptors in this case are more concerned with his own plans than with yours.

More important receptors than the brain neurons of your spouse or your competitor are the cells of your own body.Do you feel guilt? Then guilt may well be communicated to the cells of your body. You may be interfering with the effectiveness of some kidney cell receptors or some liver cell receptors.Do you feel hostility toward your competitor? That hostility could quite likely be disruptive to some cells of your body that are particularly sensitive to hostility.

The mind is constantly thinking. And its thoughts are known to the living cells in this world that are in some way involved with those thoughts. It is less important a scientific fact that the philodendron "knew" Backster was coming back to the lab as it is that your heart cells "know" you are under stress. Primary perception by living cells is almost always more demonstrable when it is a matter of life and death.

Knowing about primary perception and how our thoughts are known by our vital organ cells can be valuable knowledge in the growing understanding and acceptance of holistic approaches to health. Does a single cell know your thoughts? Research points to "yes." A single cell appears to have a primary perception enabling it to react to thoughts, especially to thoughts with high emotion or thoughts of life or death.

AN INSIDE LOOK AT THE
SECRET LIFE OF CELLS

Here is an example of a laboratory demonstration of this fact. It is just one example of hundreds that Backster has recorded. Some are high quality, others medium or low quality. This is a high quality example.

On the night of June 30, 1980, a San Diego State graduate student, Stephen White, a laboratory associate at Backster Research Foundation, agreed to monitor cells collected from his own mouth. These are commonly known as white cells. They are migratory cells that enter the mouth through the gums and perform a type of oral housekeeping.

White collected the cells from his mouth by a medically established laboratory procedure. He connected the cells to the instrumentation and turned on two video cameras, one aimed at the polygraph chart, the other at the chair in which he would sit about fifteen feet from the electroded cells. The two video images were playing simultaneously side by side on one video screen. The chart recording was activated.

Backster had no more idea about what was about to happen next, nor did White, than you the reader have at this moment.

They began to rap about the past day or two. White recalled an interesting interview with physicist William Shockley's radically controversial view on genetics. "Where did you read this interview?" Backster asked White. White thought a moment.

"*Playboy.* I don't know which issue."

"Wait. I think I know where I can find a copy," claimed Backster leaving the lab and returning a few minutes later. He handed the magazine to White. While White began flipping the pages looking for the article, Backster glanced at the polygraph chart. It was serrated with little ups and downs but basically flat.

White stopped at a certain page. Instantly there was a dramatic upheaval in the polygraph pen connected to his mouth cells fifteen feet away. A wildly swinging pen was now tearing across the chart.

White had stopped to gaze at the photo of Bo Derek in the nude.

"Hold it there," he said to White. "Keep looking at that page."

"Now take it easy, Cleve," he protested.

"I'm not ribbing you, Steve This is in the name of science."

Backster wanted to get a good lengthy read-out without risking an interrogation. White gave forth some embarrassed protests, but cooperated. Only when he closed the magazine did the chart return to its undisturbed state. (See Figure 1.)

White did not say what he was thinking. Say or not, what was going through his mind was certainly of interest to his body's cells.

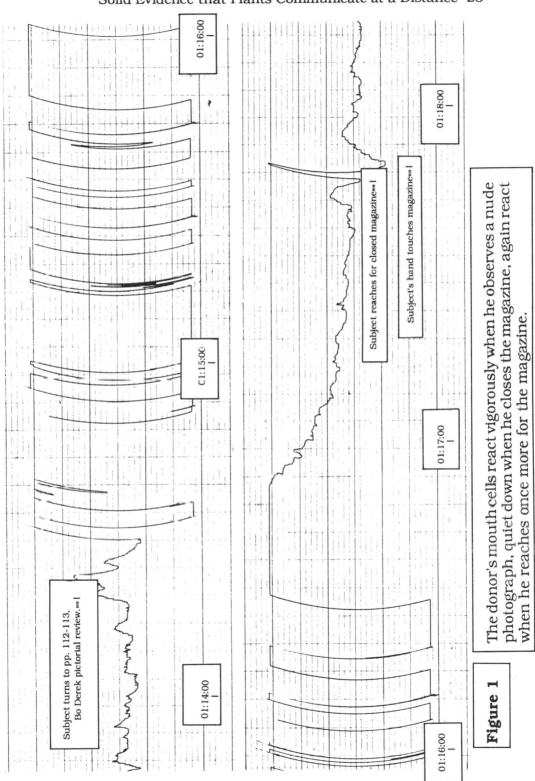

Figure 1

The donor's mouth cells react vigorously when he observes a nude photograph, quiet down when he closes the magazine, again react when he reaches once more for the magazine.

THE EQUIPMENT THAT PROVIDES
THE INSIDE LOOK

This video tape and others like it are now available for showing at the Backster Research Foundation premises to skeptical or interested scientists. Backster's goals of the past few years have been toward perfecting his equipment so that video taped conversations like these can be produced that are scrupulously professional and sophisticated.

In order to move up from the rough, amateurish quality of past tapes, he has been acquiring more advanced color video cameras and tape recorders. He also makes standard use of a "date-time generator" so that all current and future tapes will have the year, month, day, hour, minute and second printed on the screen. Also, he can now display four separate video images on the screen simultaneously. A special television microscope can video tape the reaction and movement of microbes. A time lapse recorder has also been acquired, and there is more equipment on the way.

THE KIND OF CELL PERCEPTION
CURRENTLY MEASURABLE

What does he do in the meanwhile? He makes a lot of observations and measures a lot of reactions. But one important ingredient of protocol permeates all of his activities: The mind must be kept free of protocol in the classical sense, and open to spontaneous occurrences.

Have the specific observations with White been replicated? No, and they probably never will. *That* person's mouth cells. *That* issue of *Playboy. That* picture of Bo Derek. You might substitute properly for each of the factors but can you substitute for spontaneity and consequently for reality?

This type of primary perception has been replicated scores of times, when spontaneity and reality are there.

About two years later, in 1982, Backster was being interviewed by a reporter. In order to permit some spontaneous occurrences that would demonstrate this ability of mouth cells to read our thoughts, he paid a janitor of the building five dollars to spend a few minutes with them after his day was finished.

Joe was an amiable young black man. White collected the cells from Joe's mouth, centrifuged them and connected them to the polygraph and set up the TV recording equipment and then turned on the polygraph.

They had created a small booth for their subjects which contained a large timer and a book of assorted pictures they had collected from magazines. Joe sat down next to the book and looked apprehensively at the cameras and other equipment.

"Look at these pictures, Joe," Backster instructed. "Forget about us and all the equipment. Just groove on the pictures."

He started flipping the pages. "No, Joe, it's better if you really look at each page. Take about thirty seconds before turning a page."

White, the reporter and Backster then ignored Joe and stood about fifteen feet away looking at the polygraph read-out. The pen wrote a slightly wavering line across the center of the chart paper. A floral display, a sunset, a geometrical design--no reaction. Then Joe turned the page and looked at a Marlboro ad. As he gazed at the Marlboro cowboy, the polygraph pen leaped across the page.

"He smokes Marlboros," Backster whispered to White and the reporter.

The chart pen quieted down as Joe turned the page. A well-furnished room. A large dollar sign. Stevie Wonder. Nothing.

"I don't think that's the kind of music he likes," Backster ventured to the others.

Then came a portable radio, and next a picture of ice cream sundaes. About ten or fifteen seconds into the ice cream sundaes, again the pen took a zooming climb. When he turned the page, it fell back. The next and last picture was a bare-breasted black woman. In a few seconds, the pen again went into violent motion.

Joe closed the book and got up. Backster motioned to him to join the others at the polygraph. Explaining what was being measured, Backster showed Joe the three areas where the polygraph registered excitement in his mouth cells.

"Your mouth cells know what you are thinking, Joe."Joe shook his head in disbelief.

"Let's read your thoughts right now, Joe," Backster proposed.

The very idea sent the mouth cell reaction going. The pen seemed galvanized into action. In a moment it quieted down.

"Joe," Backster said, "Think about what you and I were discussing in the elevator on the way here." It happened to be about a pretty woman. Again, the pen fairly flew across the paper.

"Thanks, Joe." Backster gave him the five dollars. "We appreciate your letting us read your thoughts."

Apparently Joe did not appreciate it. After that he refused every time he was offered the same opportunity.

THE IMPORTANT CELL MESSAGES THAT MAY SOON BE MEASURED

Can any grand conclusions be drawn from these mouth cell observations? No, except that cell perception is in evidence. But how can we use this fact of life?

Perhaps medical research in hospitals should begin observing liver cells, artery cells, heart cells, kidney cells, etc., and record what kind of thoughts most severely affect each vital organ and system.

This leads away from allopathic medicine and in the direction of holistic approaches to disease prevention and so would not generate funds from the chemical and medical manufacturers. It would probably have to be a government sponsored activity.

But, because hospital and medical bills are soaring, Medicare and Medicaid are risking financial trouble. This could be an answer for the federal government.

It could also be an answer to some incurable death-dealing diseases.

How Backster's research dovetails with other research now going on will be covered in the chapters ahead. How Soviet scientists have related to this work will also be covered. We will be examining that two-edged sword: The human mind--and we will be sticking our editorial neck way out, and suggesting how, by knowing what other human minds are thinking, we can apply this knowledge of the secret life of cells to benefit our lives starting now. First, let's start with an update on plants.

Footnotes:

[1]Harper and Row, Publishers, Inc., New York, 1973 and Avon books, New York, 1974

Chapter II

Today Plants Know Your Thoughts ...Tomorrow?

In the days of "Secret Life of Plants" Cleve Backster lived in Manhattan. This is where the plant research began and where it progressed to other forms of life.

Now he lives and works in San Diego. He has a suite of rooms on an upper floor of an eight story building on the corner of Sixth and E Streets. The laboratory occupies one of the floor's two wings, nearly 2,000 square feet. It was formerly occupied by the U.S. Drug Enforcement Agency. They are large fluorescent-lit rooms containing polygraphs, video-taping equipment, plants, aquariums, microscopes and other equipment.

In the same building is the Backster School of Lie Detection. When he is not researching, he is teaching. He also has a small penthouse apartment in the same building which serves a dual purpose. He provides the building with video equipment for security purposes and this is run from both the lab and the apartment. He also sometimes sleeps in the apartment. Sometimes, because he is a nocturnal person, he rises late in the morning, researches or teaches all afternoon and in the evening, works until 3:00 a.m. or even later.

The original Dracena Massangeana, now over twenty years old

and looking more like a tree than a plant, is located in the lab area. Seven smaller plants of this type, all cuttings from the original one provide part of the greenery in the lab work rooms.

WHAT MAKES BACKSTER RUN

It was in New York City well past the middle of the night, in fact toward morning, when Backster first got the idea to hook the polygraph to the dracena as has already been related.

What he really wanted to find out early on February 2, 1966 was how long it took for moisture to rise in the plant from root to leaf. What actually happened was very different and about to change his life and may well have set the stage for changing the lives of many others.

It led him to make so many observations with that plant in the next few hours, that by the time his business partner Bob Henson arrived he had tacked this lengthy chart on the wall of the long hallway.

"Whom have you been testing?" Henson asked.

"Reach out your hand," said Backster.

"This plant?"

Backster nodded, grinning.

Backster remembers himself as always having been an inquisitive individual, willing to stick his neck out and take chances. As a teenager, he was envious of high divers but had a fear of diving, even from a modest height, himself. At seventeen, in an attempt to rid himself of that phobia, during a water pool show he climbed to the top of a ten-meter diving tower, had someone douse his sweat pants with gasoline and then strike a match. With the pants aflame, he had no choice but to swan dive into the pool below. As a result of that incident, he did a two-summer stint in the New York Aquacade Show continued by the New York City Park Department as an aftermath of the New York World's Fair.

He enrolled in the University of Texas planning a major in Engineering. But restless in that work, he switched after one semester to agriculture at Texas A&M and later to psychology. Looking back, he sees how all three would play a role in the work he would be doing. Then came Pearl Harbor and he joined the Navy, having completed only several semesters toward bachelor's degree.

In the Navy, he aimed for Naval Intelligence.

He was interested in hypnosis and saw military applications in brainwashing which he wanted to help to counter, if possible. The Navy sent him back to school again, several schools, one being Middlebury College in Vermont in the Navy V-12 program where he took three more semesters of psychology.

In those days his exuberance was interpreted as a sign of youth.   Today, his continuing youthful enthusiasm is often deemed unbefitting to the academic and scientific approach.

After his discharge from the Navy, following the end of World War II, he switched again.   He joined the Army Counterintelligence Corps.   It was a fortunate move.   It was where he was supposed to be.   He began teaching government and military people the potential of the use of hypnosis in interrogation and how to defend themselves against its use by others.

At last, he was in his field--the field of consciousness.

HIS WORK WITH THE CIA

It also happened to be an area of interest of the Central Intelligence Agency.   They had heard about his work.   They terminated his Army enlistment in order to hire him as a civilian. There he worked on counter-interrogation techniques that gradually moved in the direction of the operational use of the polygraph.

Those were productive years but he yearned for his freedom to research outside of CIA guidelines.   In 1951, after leaving the CIA, and briefly serving as Director of the only school training polygraph examiners, he founded his own polygraph business, Backster began counseling other government agencies as well as businesses in the uses of the polygraph, and researching ways to further perfect the accuracy and dependability of the polygraph.

In 1959, he was co-founder and director of a lie detection school and in 1965 he founded the Backster Research Foundation. Then came that experience with the plant on February 2, 1966 which was to catapult him into the kind of research directions, he – and probably nobody else – had dreamed of .

In 1983 he was honored with a Life Membership from the American Polygraph Association.

What does Cleve Backster look like today? Solidly built, he has a squarish face, shaped and lined as if by a caricaturist striving to emphasize the man's intensity of involvement in his work while yet maintaining a detached scientific professionalism. That intensity also comes through in his speech, voluble and rapid when on his favorite subjects. From time to time he clears his throat, even thought it does not need clearing, a mannerism that not only gives his thoughts a chance to catch up, but the listener's as well.

COMMUNICATION WITH PLANTS
EXISTED BEFORE BACKSTER

George Washington Carver, botanist who died in 1943, discovered many uses for the peanut that turned it from a practically worthless crop into a valuable product of many uses. It is reported that he claimed that the peanuts talked to him and told him what they were good for.

Conversation with plants, both to and from did not start with the partial publication of Backster's findings in *Secret Life of Plants* or in such other publications as *Reader's Digest, McCalls, Harpers, Wall Street Journal, Christian Science Monitor*, etc., but it most assuredly took a decided jump in popularity at that time.

Today, many graduates of the Silva Mind Control training who perfect their ability to communicate subjectively by activating the right hemisphere of the brain are able to both project and detect plant information. One mushroom cultivator was able to determine why a particular batch was not thriving. She went to her relaxed level of mind where alpha brain wave frequencies are dominant and right brain output is greater.

"They say they are smothering," she said, Her partner looked into the ventilation system. Sure enough, it was blocked.

The author, who is also a Silva graduate, was asked by his wife to check out one of their house plants that seemed to be wilting. Returning from his alpha level, he said, "This is ridiculous, but the plant said it needs fish."

"What's so ridiculous," she replied, "There's a fish emulsion product for plants. I'll get it." She applied it and the plant immediately responded.

In other projects, Silva graduates have increased the growth of plant life with thought. By sending positive thoughts to one batch of mung bean sprouts, negative thoughts to another, they have observed a 50 percent increase in sprout length in the former. They have prolonged the life of a tomato with the energy of consciousness, while other tomatoes not so treated, rotted.

More formal work done with plants is covered by Bird and Tompkins in *Secret Life of Plants.* It will be cited where appropriate as we address the basic concept: We are not alone in our thoughts. Our thoughts are known by single cell organisms as well as by the cells of complete organisms, from friendly yogurt bacteria to brain neurons. They appear to act on this information. If this is so, then how can we humans harness this action for our own betterment?

Once Backster had gotten over his initial shock of plants reacting to his thoughts, he began some serious experimentation that he could pass on to interested scientific investigators.

Since the plant reacted to his thought of burning them and later to germs being killed by an antiseptic, he decided to embark on a series of experiments with brine shrimp.

COMMUNICATION RECORDED BETWEEN BRINE SHRIMP AND PLANTS

Brine shrimp are easy to handle. Brine shrimp eggs come in dried form. Put them in salt water and inside of twenty-four hours they are swimming around as tiny shrimp. But, they are not robust, healthy shrimp and are used mostly as feed for tropical fish. He used mature healthy shrimp which he purchased from a tropical fish store. His plan was to drop these adult shrimp into boiling water, thus terminating them, and recording the reactions, if any, of the polygraph-monitored plants.

The first few times he did this, he got timely reactions: the plants reacted dramatically to the demise of the shrimp. But after two or three such demonstrations, this reaction stopped. The plants seemed to tune into his thoughts as if to give these thoughts higher priority than the subtle sensitivity to the death of the brine shrimp.

He went down to the well stocked plant section of a nearby Woolworth store and bought more philodendrons. But he had to be careful just how he did this. If he were to be closely associated with the plants, there could be the capability of the plants to maintain an attunement to him more than to the shrimp. So he had another person purchase the plants from Woolworth's and place them in another part of the building that he did not frequent. Just prior to the use of the plants, he and his partner,

Robert Henson, brought the plants into the experiment area, and attached the plants to the equipment.

By clamping an electrode on each side of one of the plant leaves, thus subjecting it to the necessary contact pressure, along with the minute circuit electricity, enough "discomfort" was produced to disorient the plant and prevent it from maintaining an attunement to the two men. They set a time delay switch to allow for the start of the experiment, and quickly scooted out of the laboratory.

Only when they took such precautions in order to direct the plant's "psychological set" to its own problem in its own immediate area were they able to obtain results with the automated dropping of brine shrimp into boiling water.

PLANTS APPEAR TO ADAPT TO
THE FACT OF DEATH

These plants were used for only two, at most three, research runs. After that, it was likely that adapting would take place, and they would not react to the death of the shrimp.

If the two researchers were the least bit careless with these precautions, and had kept the plants there for a few hours, the plants appeared to become attuned to them. Then, even though they walked a full avenue away to stay away from the environment while the experiment was being run, the plants would appear to place the men's thoughts as more important than the shrimp's death. The two men learned this the hard way. Several times they waited in the lab reception area for the experiment to be concluded only to find that the plants appeared to be tuned into their conversation, not the shrimps' demise.

They had to capitalize on the plants being in a new environment, out of their element in a strange place, with a trickle of electricity going through them, and the unnatural pressure of the electrical contacts. Their equivalent of the human psychological set was really reaching out to any kind of clue to what was going on in that environment.

Then, they really latched on to the death of the brine shrimp as meaningful information input--and instrument action detected that response.

Can you imagine what it must have felt like for human beings to hear for the first time that an automobile killed a person? Now that this is repeated thousands of times a year, what else is new? The plants seemed to adapt similarly to the death of the shrimp.

PLANTS DIFFERENTIATE BETWEEN HEALTHY AND UNHEALTHY LIFE

Another factor entered the picture. The plants reacted fine if healthy brine shrimp were used. But if the brine shrimp tested were less than healthy, their demise did not seem to bother the plants at all.

Says Backster, "Differentiating between healthy and un-healthy life forms gets to be a little complicated and somewhat discouraging. But with the brine shrimp there is an easy way to select the healthy ones. They are totally dedicated to the perpetuation of their species. They are always involved in either the love chase or the love act.

"When we saw them doing this sort of thing, we caught these happily engaged couples and put them in the dump dish, knowing that we had healthy shrimp."

You would think that with all of the publicity he received in the late sixties and early seventies that there would be "cruelty" complaints, but it took four years before he got his first letter saying, "stop killing brine shrimp."

Eventually he did, but there was still more need for these shrimp. A well controlled experiment was always planned with the serious scientist in mind. There were some that gave Backster and his colleagues the hardest time. Some physicists brought up seemingly extraneous factors which they did not understand themselves, such as the identifying of the precise part of the electromagnetic spectrum involved. Backster had to protect his experiment results by not allowing good data to be discredited by careless theory.

They kept all doors closed. They used four polygraphs, each of three going to its separate plant, and the fourth going to a neutral fixed value resistor. They had a control cable that came down the hall which was spring-loaded and split so there was no possibility of a communication linkage of a conventional nature.

The random time mechanism was activated. They left, and the shrimp were later terminated in the boiling water.

To keep the recording of the results objective, his associate Robert Henson, participated during all of the final experiment runs so that nobody could accuse Backster of manipulating the results.

Success followed success.

When they tested three plants at a time, they got several double "hits" and a possible triple "hit." The overall results were statistically significant. The series of plants kept reacting.

As these results were published first in a scientific journal, and then in magazines, Backster was bombarded with requests for protocol and results. He filled thousands of such requests. National Wildlife magazine reported that readership interest and response broke all records, exceeding any item that ever appeared in their magazine.

Electrotechnology magazine did a short summary of the research. The circulation of this magazine was to engineers and senior design scientists in large corporations, government agencies, and universities. They considered a high response to be one thousand inquiries. The article about his work received over five thousand inquiries, even though it had the nonscientific title "Do Plants Feel Emotion?"

DO PLANTS HAVE EMOTIONS?

"I never say anything about emotions in plants. But people say it for me," claims Backster.

"Similarly, I do not always learn from structured experiments. I emphasize high quality observation. What happens, happens." Backster likes to pepper his theory talk with real life examples:

"In those days, I had a Doberman pincher dog. I kept him in the lab area. I would supplement his standard dog food with an egg, removing the white and putting the yolk in, supposedly good for the coat.

"One day I broke an egg for the dog food and noticed something out of the side of my eye.

"A polygraph was monitoring a plant about fifteen or twenty feet away. I had arranged a meter on the wall so I could see possible reactions wherever I happened to be standing.

"When I broke the egg, the meter waved violently. Since I saw it only peripherally, I resolved to watch it more carefully on the next occasion.

"The next day, when it came time to feed the dog, I kept my eye on this meter which had been rather calm for a period of time. The moment I cracked the egg, swish, that meter went into wild gyrations." (See Figure 2.)

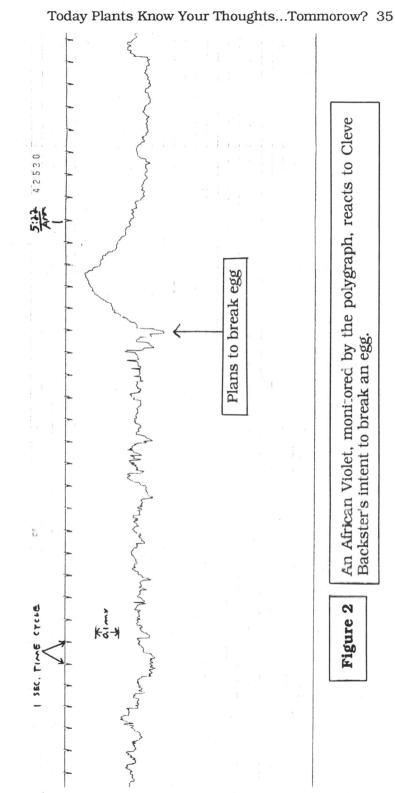

Figure 2   An African Violet, monitored by the polygraph, reacts to Cleve Backster's intent to break an egg.

You can believe that the third egg did not have to wait for the following day.

Not only did the plants react to the demise of the egg, but the egg reacted to its own impending demise.

Later he found that the eggs he had bought were not fertile eggs. So he obtained some fertile eggs. Fertile or unfertile, the eggs reacted to his thoughts of breaking them.

This was the breakthrough that caused Backster to experiment with forms of life other than plants.

DISCOVERIES ABOUT THE SECRET LIFE OF CELLS HAD TO REMAIN SECRET

Before going into details of this other work and their implications relative to cells having a communications ability, our social state of consciousness in those days needs to be appreciated.

Here Backster was making earth-shaking observations, but he had to be careful about "disclosing" them at this stage.

The plants appeared to be safe enough. With the plants there were not as many alternate explanations as with other forms of life.

Every discipline of science required controlled repeatable experiments, ignoring dozens of high quality observations that pointed to a clear pattern. But because that clear pattern did not fit an existing paradigm within scientific knowledge, it was ignored.

This requirement to "jump through the hoop" is a perversion of the scientific method, but there it is. It can be observed in law, medicine, and other professions. But it is most stifling when scientists toe the "status quo" line.

If Backster had shared with others some of the effects he then began to observe in animal cells and discussed their obvious medical implications, he would have been slaughtered by the medical profession. A reflex action would have taken place to defend their position. This would have meant slug Backster first and look into it later, if at all.

He would not have been the first to suffer such treatment. His disaster would be lost in the statistics of such tactics.

Less so today. Holistic health approaches have made inroads into the allopathic monopoly. A new breed of young doctors recognize the mind-body connection. The effect of stressful thoughts on vital organs a foot or two away from the brain, which is the source of these stressful thoughts, are recognized. Information on just how these biochemical communications take place would be more readily accepted.

Again, if Backster had jumped into the theological implications, he could have gotten just as badly hurt.

Up until February 1966 when that plant reacted to his thoughts, Backster was agnostic. He was agnostic only because he had not taken the trouble to be an atheist.

For fourteen years of his childhood, he had been compelled to attend Sunday School and church each Sunday. His father was superintendent of that Presbyterian Sunday School for nearly thirty years. He attended fourteen years without missing a Sunday and was awarded a wreath and thirteen attached bars for that perfect record.

But he had an inquisitive mind. He would hear religious things on Sunday and then on Monday he would hear from more scientific sources that it was not true.

This created a conflict within him. He did not know what to believe.

When the plant reacted to his sincere intention to burn it but did not react when he made believe that he was going to burn it, he saw the connection between that and the statement he heard in church: insincere prayer never leaves the lips of the person praying.

Suddenly, he saw a connection between all living things. The Good Book had said something about oneness and the attunement of all things. Could this oneness that he was recording be part of that vaguely expressed manifestation of God?

Can you imagine what would happen to him in those days had he made some religious utterance along those lines?

THESE SECRETS CAN NOW BE DIVULGED

But times are changing. Call it "The Greening of America" or "The Aquarian Conspiracy" or something else, there is an opening of minds toward matters still beyond the reach of conventional science and organized religion. New physics, new thought, new approaches are less threatening to people than they used to be.

People ask Backster how many "kook" letters he has received in the past twenty-three years. "What do I use as a standard?" he replies. "How do I identify a `kook' letter?"

Years ago, he might have said that most of the letters he would later be receiving were "kook" letters. He would have thought most of the people who wrote him were "nuts." Today, as he looks at these letters, none of them are "kook" letters, with rare exception. What seems to be "far out" in the past days can be the "in" thing today. Most people who were called "kooks" were really not "kooks," but rather more like pacesetters. Says Backster, "The real `kooks' might well be the people who were doing the name calling."

. Certainly humanity is readier today than it was a decade or two ago for the concept of a "connection" that unites living cells on all levels, perhaps even readier than it is for atomic energy.

Hence the timing of this book.

THE MEANING TO US ALL OF INTELLIGENCE IN CELLS

Science has been moving in the direction of acknowledging a continuum of intelligence in space.

Religions have been moving in the direction of the universality of a Higher Intelligence.

Neither will likely attempt to crucify Backster as they might have years ago.

So he shares on these pages some of the remarkable events ever experienced – intelligence at work in ways that may help confirm our theology or philosophy if we have one, or tempt us to embrace one, if we don't.

Here is what it may well boil down to. We are likely all accountable. We cannot go into an alley or other secluded place where we don't think anyone will see us and do something abusive and think we are getting away with it.

Privacy seems now to be non-existent. It appears to be an illusion. How can there be privacy, if everything is connected through a oneness, a continuum of intelligence, a morphogenetic field, a collective unconscious or anything else you want to call it? Your secret thoughts are communicated to every cell in your body and probably to a larger continuum of intelligence in space.

When it comes to your movements, your whereabouts, your thoughts, there appears to be nothing that even resembles a secret. The so-called Backster Effect, the Remote Viewing ability, and other observable phenomena all seem to agree: it is likely that you are not alone. How can there ever be invasion of privacy should privacy be non-existent?

The world today might be suddenly free of many of its problems if people en masse realize that they are automatically accountable for their actions.

Yes, Backster attached polygraphs to plants but in the process, he found plants attached to him. His older plants appear more interested in his comings and goings than in the survival of brine shrimp.

"While plant recordings were occurring in the lab," Backster explains, "I began to carry a stopwatch around with me wherever I went. If there was a sudden decision to return to the laboratory--maybe I got a telephone message or the like--I would activate the stopwatch at that instant. Then when I arrived back at the laboratory and checked the charts, a plant reaction had indeed taken place at that precise time of my decision to return to the lab.

"Futhermore, the attunement to the researcher destroyed all interest on the plant's behalf in the brine shrimp. Whereas the plant may have reacted sharply to the automated dumping of the brine shrimp into boiling water, if it had not been kept for several days in the lab, no such reaction took place."

Think of all abilities and characteristics on display here.

It points to plant memory.

It suggests plant priority-oriented affinity for a particular life form.

It implies the plant's ability to transcend the barriers of distance.

It demonstrates the plant's ability to discriminate between two inputs, select the one of greatest importance, and screen out the other.

Suddenly the ability of the flycatcher plant to trap insects and the other "thinking" traits of plants toward surviving in their natural habitat do not appear to be the miracles of nature that they once seemed to be.

When we see such behavior in the context of memory, attachment, perception, awareness and feeling, it becomes almost expected.

THE SECRET LOVE LIFE OF CELLS

A whole field yet to be explored is what plants might emit as senders to us. Following up on Backster's work with plants in New York City, an International Business Machines scientist in

Los Gatos, California, Marcel Vogel, was discovering that his thoughts could affect the growth of plants.

Three leaves, picked from an elm outside his IBM laboratory, were laid on a piece of glass next to his bed. Each morning, when he awoke, Vogel would concentrate on the two outer leaves, exhorting them to live, sending them mental support, while totally ignoring the center leaf. In seven days, that center leaf had withered and turned brown while the two outer leaves were still green and healthy.

Vogel went on to replicate many of Backster's observations and to expand the work in other directions. For instance, with a plant connected to a galvanometer producing a flat read-out, he would relax through deep breathing and extend his hands toward the plant without actually touching it. He would then feel love and affection for the plant, showering it so to speak with tender thoughts.

The chart would show an immediate reaction by the plant. The recording pen would record a series of higher and higher oscillations. At the same time, Vogel's palms recorded an output from the plant. It felt like a form of energy and lasted three to five minutes. It felt as if they were lovers.

With two plants wired up, Vogel snipped a leaf from the first plant. The second plant reacted, but only if Vogel was paying attention to the second plant.

You might have to be a psychologist to analyze that reaction. At any rate, Vogel was seeing a new type of love triangle.

Love can very well be the common denominator of all of this communication. It could be the "gravitational field" of the non-physical continuum we call the oneness.

But can you see the scientific world investigating love?

They are having a hard enough time with consciousness.

There was a time when consciousness was not recognized by scientists. It could not be measured. Now it is being associated with energy and how that energy of consciousness is able to affect matter is being likened to the way plasma affects magnetic lines of force. An association of psychotronic researchers has been meeting every two years in different locations around the world. Physicists, chemists, biologists and scientists in just about every discipline share the results of their research into the energetic effects of consciousness.

We are getting there.

ENTER: PRIMARY INTELLIGENCE

Here is something else seen in the laboratory that makes one stop and think.

We referred to how plants adapt to death or destruction of life forms, such as the brine shrimp. After two or three repetitions, they no longer show any interest in the death of brine shrimp or after such repetitions with other life forms. There is one exception: human cells. Let Backster explain:

"I cut my finger. The plant reacted. It reacted again when I put iodine on the cut. Every time I cut my finger accidentally, the plant reacted. It did not adapt to the death of human cells.

"Frankly, that was a bit of a shock to me. Is there something special about human life? Are we sort of at the top of the heap, hierarchy wise? If so, what happens to that concept of oneness?"

plants depend on man

It may be a ways down the road before the answer to that one is known. We may be interpreting the adapting reaction wrongly. Certainly what should override the plants' adapting phenomena is the universality of life from humans on down through dogs, insects, tiny shrimp, and even further.

In New York City, Backster was recording reactions during the day that he could not explain. He would be experiencing rather tranquil tracings without too much variation when all of the sudden the tracing practically leaped off the chart paper with no apparent reason.

It took a while, but he discovered the cause. There was a men's lavatory on the other side of the wall. Just prior to the sound of flushing of a urinal, the plant reacted very violently. There was a definite correlation between the use of the lavatory facilities and these reactions. On further investigation, he found that they used a strong disinfectant in the urinals. Living cells in the body's excretion, and there are thousands, were being terminated by the disinfectant. Also, the temperature change appeared to be factor.

When a person visiting the lab used the restroom facilities but was aware of this fact, the reactions ceased.

Let's examine these two observations: One, the plants react when living cells are terminated by a combination of the urinal's disinfectant and temperature change. Two, when a human mind expects this to happen, the plants no longer react. Is it possible the mind is then preparing the cells for their fate?

Furthermore, Backster can detach a leaf from a plant, connect the separated leaf to the polygraph and still get the reactions that he had been getting from the whole plant.

Now, please hang on to your seat. Backster can grind the leaf up into tiny particles, put the particles between the polygraph electrodes and obtain the same reactions he could receive from the whole leaf and the whole plant.

When laser light hits a matrix and a hologram is projected out into space, no matter where on the matrix it hits, the whole picture is produced. It hits only a relatively few molecules, yet the full out-picturing takes place.

We see a parallel in primary perception. It is as if a primary intelligence is present.

The purported tooth of Buddha is worshipped in Kandi Temple in Bali. Elsewhere, the same adoration is shown toward hair and nail cuttings of some respected person. Instinctively, man knows that the part represents the whole.

We need to understand primary perception.

With this understanding, there may come benefits to mankind that we cannot yet comprehend, much less predict.

This understanding of the secret abilities of cells may well enable us to better control our relationships with germs, with vital organs, with other people.

It could open up abilities, now lying dormant within us, to control our health and happiness. We have billions upon billions of tiny friends waiting for the word from us to get into the "ball game," on our side.

We are going to be considering how we can give that word.

Chapter III
Scope of Plant Sensitivity

The 1988 summer drought caused plants to literally "cry out" for water. As they withered they made sounds pitched too high for human ears to hear (thank nature for that; imagine the pain and misery such noises would otherwise cause us), but not out of reach of electronic monitoring devices which Agriculture Department researchers used.

As water stopped moving from roots to leaves, cell structures and capillaries broke down. It was presumably this destructive process that could be electronically "heard."

This was the fifth year that the researchers have been studying these "sounds" with the potential benefit sought of being able to let irrigation farmers know just when to water their fields, and also to help them develop new plant varieties which would be better able to move water and its nutrients in near drought conditions.

There is something too pat about the breaking down of cells as an explanation of electronic communication. Heisenberg once said, "What we observe is not nature itself, but nature exposed to our method of questioning."

Question instead whether the plants are broadcasting a perception of their impending demise, a sort of biological SOS, and the explanation that emerges may be less a breakdown of cell structure and more The Backster Effect.

"E Pluribus Unum" which appears on the seal of the United States – check the one dollar note – means in effect: from many, one. The founding fathers saw this applicable to the many states forming one union. However, among them were a few metaphysicians who "felt" the destiny of this country and saw it leading other countries into an international community, or one world. Their support for the adoption of this phrase to be part of the seal came from their concept of an ultimate togetherness that was the idea masked by separation throughout the universe.

Fritjof Capra writes, "Quantum Theory forces us to see the universe not as a collection of physical objects, but rather as a complicated web of relations between the various parts of a unified whole.[1]"

Plant communication when viewed not as a part contacting another part, but as one of the functions of the unified whole, then becomes quite a different matter.

Yes, electronic equipment can tap into it and be affected by it, and yes, it can be viewed as an energetic process similar to wave propagation and modulation.

But no, it is not really what that approach makes it appear to be. That approach is a method of questioning which compels that response. Other methods of questioning could evoke a different response.

Suppose the questioner had a consciousness of unity behind separations. Suppose he or she assumed a fundamental field of intelligence that filled all space, as other fields do.

Electronic equipment would then become one tool in the research. The primary perception of plants would merely be the "part" acting as the "whole." And what Backster is really demonstrating is the existence not only of a primary perception at the plant cell level but a primary intelligence at the plant cell level.

WE GET ANSWERS THAT FIT THE QUESTIONS

If we were to examine some of the ingenious activities in which plants engage – and we will in a moment – in the light of not just a primary perception but also a primary intelligence, we are immediately less astounded.

It is a comfortable concept. It is like extrapolating from the concept that 30 million brain neurons can come up with one single thought, to the concept that a plant is one "neuron" in the universal "mind."

As we observe plants adapting to the environment in ingenious ways, do we question how it is done with an open mind or with Darwin's mind? With Darwin's mind, we get back Darwinian explanations, which boil down to the plant's having tried out multifarious approaches to survive in the environment and this is the one that succeeded – survival of the fittest.

The answer becomes a direct function of our mode of questioning.

Should our mode of questioning instead be one that assumes a primary perception and even a primary intelligence, we are bound to get back explanations that point to that very primary intelligence.

So where is one approach any more valid than the other?

It isn't. But there is more and more basis for believing that there is a non-physical cause to this physical effect we call the universe. Past ages have produced different and often conflicting pictures of the universe, each of which has been superseded by another.

Today the concept that is accepted with increasing universality is one of there being a continuum of intelligence that fills all space. It is the only concept that can explain some of the abilities that are observed under laboratory conditions, especially of the human mind. Take these three examples:

Remote viewing is an on going research. Men and women are able to describe events and places hundreds of miles away chosen by random computer.

Absent healing is an on-going activity participated in by the Unity Church as well as Silva Mind Control graduates, and so-called "new thought" groups.

Subjective communication, once referred to as mental telepathy, is fast becoming an on-going tool of consciousness in society and the business world.

Can these abilities be traced to our genes? Or are they likely the workings of a larger intelligence of which we are part? And is this larger intelligence the ultimate oneness?

Skeptics cringe at the latter explanation. It comes too close to authenticating religion. It is a fundamental philosophy of classical scientists that they must check their brains at the door if entering a church. Words that come close to enunciating Creator are a scientific no-no.

But plants have a say in the matter.

DO PLANTS HAVE A HIGH I.Q.?

In September of 1974, Daphne Beall, a mathematics instructor for eight years at Yuba College in Marysville, California, performed an experiment with tomatoes in Guam to where she had recently moved.

She filled a container with water and then energized the water by placing her hands around it without touching it, going to a relaxed state of mind, and visualizing energy leaving her hands in the form of a white light and entering the water. She imagined the water becoming whiter and brighter as a sign of it being energized. She did this for ten minutes.

She then took an ordinary tomato, immersed it in the charged water and left it there overnight. As a control she did the same with another tomato in plain water. Both were taken out of the water in the morning and put on separate plates.

Within three to four days, the tomato that had been in the ordinary water began to shrivel. It shriveled more and more each day, becoming smaller and smaller. The tomato in the charged water remained healthy for eight days. It, too, began to leak but then appeared to heal itself and the leaking stopped. It remained healthy for a second week, but then developed a split in its skin, but did not leak. Once again the tomato appeared to heal itself, the break in the tomato's skin beginning to look like a half-healed cut in human skin. That tomato did not begin to deteriorate until the end of three weeks.

Since then this demonstration has taken place many times and the "tomato experiment" has become a classic, starting in Silva circles and being adopted by teachers at all levels.

What is happening? What is the life extension factor at work here? Given the following possible explanations, which would you vote for?

(a) Humans have the ability to project life energy into each other and other life forms.

(b) Plants not only have the innate ability to synthesize light energy for their growth but also psychotronic energy (the energy of consciousness.)

(c) Coincidence.

(d) Plants are intelligent enough to take advantage of the special condition (charged water) and use it for their benefit.

(e) None of the above.

I cannot argue with (a) but it seems a limited concept of a larger phenomenon. Where does this energy come from? As to (b), plants have grown outside the range of human consciousness, how can they suddenly acquire a new synthesizing skill? In (c), we assume coincidence after coincidence after coincidence which in itself is an impossible coincidence. Plant intelligence, credited in (d), is an assumption that is partially true but which has its limits. Even Backster hesitated at using that concept of intelligence in his plant research. Now that the research has progressed to animal cells there is even more reticence in crediting intelligence to the cells and more validity sticking to the term perception.

Which leaves (c). And that's where my vote goes.

Why look for a source of intelligence in plants when they live in a field of intelligence? We may spend billions of dollars looking for cellular "brains," neurological connectors, biological channels, chemical reactions, and electronic signals, only to find that the original source of creation is still present,--and at work.

SOME ASTOUNDING "INTELLIGENCE" SHOWN BY PLANTS

Experiments at the University of Ottawa in the mid-60s found that ultrasonic frequencies could stimulate growth in some plants and inhibit it in others.

Subsequently, evidence of a more anecdotal nature has repeatedly indicated a preference by plants for classical music toward which they turn and grow and an apparent dislike for hard rock from which they turn away. Intelligence or instinct?

How much technology do we need to smash an atom? How many human brains are there in the world today that can create the necessary equipment and administer it to its energy-releasing, matter-converting conclusion? Not many, but...

A blade of grass can do it.

A plant grown in distilled water showed no change in its phosphorus or potassium content, but when grown in a calcium salt solution, it varied that content by as much as 10 percent. Pierre Baranger, director of the organic chemistry laboratory at the prestigious Ecole Polytechnique in Paris, used every precaution in his experiments but had to conclude that plants know the secrets of alchemy and are transmuting elements under our very eyes.

Knowing this, it is easy to accept the fact that plants can become shaped to accommodate the insects that they depend upon for pollination, and even take on the colors to which such insects are most sensitive.

Other plants, that consume insects like the flycatcher, engage in wily entrapments. In others, roots seem to "know" in which direction to find water. Leaves go through maze-like journeys to reach the sun. Barks of trees produce a defensive chemical when a certain predator is present.

Yet, if plants were given the standard I.Q. test they would, of course, flunk.

What then do we use to locate, identify , and measure plant intelligence?

INTELLIGENCE: A PROPERTY
OF PLANTS OR OF NATURE?

In the 1970s the community of Findhorn in northern Scotland created a sensation. A bleak, barren peninsula became a tropical-like garden. The size of its vegetables and the beauty of its blossoms, some of which grew out of season, were the talk of "new thought" circles. Here was thought in action. Here was proof that the mind could do the "impossible."

Findhorn community builders used all the standard agricultural methods to create healthy plants, but one additional ingredient was added to the recipe: The intelligence of nature was invoked.

Findhorn people communicated regularly with nature through the energies or entities that God had placed in charge of growing plants. The soil was transformed as their plants grew. The food was transformed. As a result, they were transformed.

The focus became on how to create a healthful environment and how to live in balance and harmony with it.

George Washington Carver claimed to have spoken to plant intelligences all his life – the then lowly peanut telling him of all the uses to which it could be put, and ultimately was. But were Carver's so-called plant intelligences really the intelligences of a different and probably larger source?

About 60 miles south of Washington, D.C. and to the west is a 22-acre garden named Perelandra. It is a "Center for Nature Research" in the genre of Findhorn. Its founder and manager is Machaelle Small Wright. She purportedly talks with animals-- there are no insect problems in her gardens – appeals to nature spirits and what she calls "overlighting intelligences still consciously connected with God."

In dry times, neighboring gardens look straggly but Perelandra keeps its vitality. Old timers in the area are stumped by Wright's successes. They lose a quarter of their cabbage to cabbage worm yearly.--she loses none. They spend large sums to combat pests. She spends nothing.

One crop that has been produced at Perelandra is a line of books and tapes to satisfy the envy of those who experience the garden. One book title is *Behaving As If The God In All Life Mattered.*[2]

Those who would measure the Perelandra success in terms of gardening technique could find plenty of grist for their mill.

Those who would measure it in terms of biological nutrition would find the chemical approaches non-existent but organic approaches quite abundant to justify their approach.

Those who would measure it in terms of human intelligence working in partnership with a higher intelligence would nod in awe.

Those who would measure it in terms of plant intelligence would have a difficult case to prove.

Certainly plant intelligence is in the picture. The cells in plants must have a primary perception keen enough to respond to a gardener's assist, to proper nutrition, to human caring, and to the "force" whatever nature's unseen partner might be called.

If we wished to examine that plant intelligence where would we look? Where is the seat of that intelligence? Are we not obliged to call it cell intelligence? Plant intelligence then becomes the collective intelligence of its cells.

HUMANS WITHER UNDER STRESS
BUT GRAPES APPEAR TO THRIVE

An Australian researcher stuck a phonograph needle into a dry castor plant and heard the plant respond with high frequency sounds. That was some 20 years ago. Now, similar sounds are being heard "through the grapevine," undoubtedly related to the drought sounds we discussed earlier.

Grapevines are being purposely stressed by giving them insufficient water. Then stress is measured by electrical signals amplified by audio emissions equipment. As compared to grapevines receiving adequate water, the grapes from the stressed vines make wine with a better aroma, flavor and appearance.

This research, being conducted by Prof. Mark Matthews and his wife Rie Ishii Matthews at the University of California, was the subject of a paper they presented to the American Society of Enology and Viticulture which has an on-going interest in water control in the vineyard.

Producers of premium wines must be certain of how much vineyard water is too much and how much is too little. The fact that too little seems to produce wine that looks, tastes and smells better is a matter of economic importance.

To us, it is a matter of philosophical importance.

Human cells appear to suffer from stress. The white cell count of a person under severe or prolonged stress goes down. That is, the person's immune system is proportionately less effective. Stress is now understood to be the cause of a broad spectrum of human illness.

If good taste, bouquet, and appearance are interpreted to mean a healthier grape, stress would appear to benefit the health of a vine.

If this is true, why would a higher form of life be less resilient to stress? Do humans have a stress-related lesson to learn from grapes, other than: wine can be a stress-reliever at the end of a difficult day?

In the pecan-growing areas of our southeast states, growth of the plants is often stimulated by flailing with sticks.

Can a stressful threat to survival be a life stimulus to plants and a life depressant to humans? If so, why?

Let's go back to the vineyards where researchers are regulating water to produce better grapes.

If the reader was of like mind with most people before beginning this book, he or she believed that a scientist was an unbiased observer conducting, but not part of, the experiment.

Can you believe that now? Only with great difficulty. It is unlikely to conceive of an energetic source of consciousness like a human being not being a factor.

The vineyard researchers are a factor. Their thoughts and feelings are perceived by the vines. The turning down of the flow of water is done, not with malice but with love. Can it be that the positive response of the vines is not from stress, but from the conscious support of the scientists that are seeking a positive effect?

Similarly, the pecans do not respond positively to negative beatings. They perceive the conscious support of the humans beating them. Can it be that their positive response is a result of that support?

Stress, then, is in the eye of the beholder. As we humans perceive events, so do our cells. As we perceive them as a threat, so are we threatened. If we perceive them as a challenge, so are we challenged. Or, as the saying goes, when the going gets tough, the tough get going.

As we perceive difficult, trying events as positive growth experiences provided by a caring natural intelligence, what will that do to our life expectancy?

And would we not also enjoy what tastes better and smells better and looks better?

More about our stress response later. Back to plants...

PLANTS GO INTO A DEAD FAINT

When Backster was doing his initial plant research, he decided to visit Dr. J.P. Rhine, the "father" of ESP (extra-sensory perception), who might provide Backster with some answers.

On the way into the building where he was to meet with Rhine, Backster took 25 or 30 leaves from a bush at the entrance. He knew that there was to be some experiments with playing cards, "guessing" whether a black or red card would be turned up next.

Equipment was set up and the leaves were to be tested with electrodes. A dish of water and a dish of acetone were placed alongside. If the card turned up was black, the leaf being tested would be put in water as a reward. If the card turned up was red, the leaf being tested would be put in acetone – a quick life terminator.

After the second leaf was put in the acetone, all the leaves went into a state of shock or fainting. That is, there would be no reaction on the equipment, neither up nor down, only a straight line.

Backster had seen this phenomenon before. On one occasion, when a person stood by to watch simple plant reactions and that person was involved as a plant physiologist with destroying plants, the plant ceased putting out measurable reactions. It went into a dead faint, similar to a state of shock in human beings. This scientist routinely roasted plants in a lab oven to obtain their dry weight.

In some cases, there was an initial mistrust, then it would either rally or not. It was as if nature has a protective device that prevents suffering.

In commenting later on this "fainting" of the leaves when a red card was turned, Backster wrote Rhine, "It seems that as a result of our experiments to date, this is not extra-sensory. It is a primary perception that is before the specialized senses. So, extra-sensory seems like a misnomer."

Backster did not know that Rhine was the one who coined that term. It was the beginning of the end of that relationship.

But Backster had good reason for his statement. He ground up a leaf and smeared it on sterile gauze, put it back between the electrodes and repeated the observations with the same results obtained previously with a whole leaf. Since this was highly suggestive of the capacity of being at the cellular level, it had to be more fundamental than the five basic senses. In other words, primary perception had to be there first.

Because plants do not have the five basic senses enjoyed by humans, they react measurably to this primary perception. What Rhine's work was attempting to prove was that when humans got their five basic senses out of the way, they too could use this primary perception!

Call it ESP, psychic function, or what you will; it was still that universally cell-pervading primary perception.

THE SOURCE OF PRIMARY
PERCEPTION IN PLANTS

British researcher Sir Oliver Lodge wrote, "We are rising to the conviction that we are part of nature, and so a part of God;...that the whole creation is traveling together toward some great end; and that now, after ages of development, we have at length become conscious portions of the great scheme and can cooperate in it with knowledge and with joy."

Apparently, even individual plant cells had risen to this conviction long before humankind, and certainly the plant itself, as an organism, was exhibiting this unity with all life before the human being as an organism was doing so.

Backster chose two plants and set them side by side in a room. One was to be destroyed. The other was to be "witness" to the crime. Six students, out of Backster's eight, drew lots to see which would be the "murderer." They picked slips of paper from a hat and one of those slips gave directions for the "murder" of the plant. The other five students left the room while the "murderer" ripped the plant out of its pot and tore it to pieces.

Backster returned, attached the remaining plant to the polygraph, and called the students. There was a flat response to the entrance of each student, but when the "murderer" entered the needle swung wildly. The surviving plant appeared to "recognize" the guilty one.

Let's examine this "recognition."

What was being recognized?

Was it the guilty student's features? Clothing? Physical profile? Odor? Characteristic movement? Some other physical trait? Or was it the guilty student's expectancy of being detected?

Each of these questions invite a five-basic-human-senses response, and so must invoke a "no."

What would invoke a "yes?" Some factor that transcends the senses. One cannot argue with "primary perception" as a satisfactory answer. But what is primary perception?

To answer that question, we must not only transcend the senses but we also transcend science in its present stage. We are forced to stand shoulder to shoulder with Sir Oliver Lodge: We have a primary perception. Plants have a primary perception. Cells have a primary perception. All because "we are part of nature, and so part of God."

SEMANTICS IN SCIENTIFIC STATEMENT

That great noise you just heard was not the echo of the big bang of creation, but the sound of thousands of scientific doors slamming in the author's face.

Scientists are "hung up" on semantics. They could possibly buy "a field of intelligence" or a "continuum of energy." But, "God?" Hell, no.

The success of plant geneticist Dr. Derald Langham began shortly after he finished a Ph.D. at Cornell University in 1939 and accepted a position in Venezuela to develop strains of sesame that would help make that country more self-sufficient. For his efforts, he received the highest decoration ever given to a foreigner – The Order of Merit in Performance – and sesame remains a leading cash crop in Venezuela today.

Langham has admitted that he owed his success to the fact that, as a boy, he could stand silently by a tree, close his eyes, and sense everything around him, even birds flying above. He used this skill with the sesame. He walked into a field with thousands of segregated groups of sesame and asked, in effect, "Which of you can best resist winds, shortage and excess of water and have a high oil content?" He would then be attracted by one or more of the segregated groups and they turned out to be the superior groups, saving him months and maybe years of standard tests and gene research.

His explanation of this ability revolved around "energy fields." He understood that by clearing his consciousness of the usual thoughts about himself and the plants, his energy field and the plants' energy field became similar or in synchronization.

At that moment, ideas came to him. Sometimes they came in a few words, like "I'm the hardiest. Over here." When he was in good sync, he sometimes got sesame communication in whole paragraphs, like "Look for ripe seeds in a green pod." He looked even though it was an illogical approach, and it was so.

We need a new language. Not illogical, but non-logical.

Allopathic medicine may continue to support chemical companies instead of the human race until acceptable nomenclature is created for alternative approaches that do not affront their principles.

No matter what branch of science one singles out, there are valid concepts outside of its accepted parameters which unite that branch with such currently disassociated approaches as philosophy and religion--pieces of the ultimate jigsaw puzzle. But these concepts are rejected out of hand. They tend to unite instead of delineate, and that is a threat to vested interests, who do not want the boundary lines of their fields of expertise blurred.

Can you really blame these experts? A cardiologist wants to be recognized as such. Should holistic approaches be accepted, his recognition is diminished.

These boundary lines are basically semantic. We have created – and are still creating – language that separates.

"Darling," a wife tells her cancer-ridden husband, "See yourself perfect. See yourself getting rid of the cancer." It is a natural appeal to make, but she is, in fact, practicing psychoneuroimmunology, one of our newest medical semantic separators.

We need a new language that unites instead of separates. The author does not pretend to have one ready to pull out of his back pocket, but if humankind's consciousness continues to become more unity-oriented, such a language is bound to emerge.

Primary perception – both the concept and the words – can be a good beginning.

SCIENCE IMPRISONED BY A MATERIAL WORLD

All the separations of science from astronomy to zoology are slices of the material world pie. Problem: The pie is entirely sliced, so where do we go now?

Not to worry. Yes, science has penetrated beyond the smallest particle within the atom and out to the farthest reaches of space. Inward or outward, no more separations are evident. Both directions lead to systems of intelligence – oneness. But...

Now, an astronautical engineer trained at the Massachusetts Institute of Technology has reported in *Sky and Telescope* [3] that a new universe of material world divisions is evident.

The "universe as atom" theory, Eugene F. Mallove explains, is now being seriously considered by cosmologists. Could the universe as we know it, be really a mere atom in a giant's teacup and can that teacup be but a speck in an even larger universe?

We previously mentioned the Big Bang. What is now theorized is that the Big Bang was not the beginning. Distant out realms sent us light via the inflation of space itself. Other conditions were supplied by this inflation of space to make the Big Bang possible. Thus the inflation of space concept gets around a difficult question faced by Big Bang theorists: If the Big Bang was the beginning, what caused the Big Bang? In other words, somehow all the points in the universe started to expand at the same instant and uniformly before there could have been any communication.

But with space inflation, we have a new beginning. and we also have a new end, for the cosmos is about to be conceived as self-reproducing. This could mean an infinitely large hierarchy of universes. "Could" because the inflation theory compels the assumption that the universe contains a critical density of matter on the border between future collapse and infinite expansion.

For the sake of us all, especially the scientists, let us pull together in the direction of infinite expansion.

SOME HUMAN-LIKE ATTRIBUTES OF PLANTS

In Backster's Times Square experiments with plant reactions, a pattern emerged.

There were reactions that implied plant memory. This is not news to plant physiologists as they see plants adapting to new surroundings. Some do not want to attribute this to memory as it brings up other problems, such as where is the seat of this memory? So they slip out by attributing this adaptation to other factors.

For Backster, on the other hand, there was no escape. Plants had to have a memory mechanism to "recognize" him after a brief time in each other's presence.

They also "remembered" experiences. Backster had a system to insure spontaneity in testing plant reaction to his point of returning to the lab while on a walk. He randomly chose one of six tapes when he left. Each had a beep that told him to return, but each was at a different elapsed time. After continued use, when he returned to the lab he began to find plant reaction at all six beep times, regardless of which tape he actually took on his walk.

Was this a type of memory? How would you like the job of locating the seat of the memory?

Plants also have the ability to respond to love. They grow better. Dwarfism has been attributed to lack of love. Place these children in a more loving parental environment and growth accelerates. So this same response in plants can be said to be a human-like attribute.

How would you like to research that particular attribute and discover the cause-effect relationships involved? You do not need a lab. Use mung bean sprouts. Put the beans in two glasses with the same amount of water and stand the glasses in the same place in your kitchen so there are no other variables than this one: From time to time during the day, visualize the right hand glass and send your love to those beans. Ignore the left. Then check the difference in growth in 24 hours. The loved beans sprout and grow twice as fast.

Suppose now you had to stand in front of a group of hard-nosed scientists and explain what you had just seen happen in your kitchen time and time again. How would you explain it? And how would they take your explanation?

You can appreciate the courage of individuals like biologist Rupert Sheldrake and researcher Cleve Backster. They appear repeatedly before different groups, on separate occasions, using their new language with terms like morphogenetic field and primary perception – rising above the need to give human-like attributes to plants and instead giving god-like attributes to both humans and plants.

A DISCRIMINATING CAPABILITY IN PLANTS

When one observes a plant's ability to discriminate in its reactions, one is sore put to conceive it as a lesser form of life.

While still in the Times Square area and experimenting with his plants' reactions to dropping live shrimp into boiling water, Backster was asked, "Why doesn't your plant react to live shrimp being put into boiling water at any one of the many Chinese restaurants in the area?"

Distance was not the answer, because the plants reacted to Backster's thoughts and actions even when he was miles away. What Backster began to see was that his plants reacted only when their own well-being was affected in some meaningful way.

If Backster himself purchased the plants at Woolworth's up the street, brought them back to the lab, hooked them up to the polygraph, and himself watered them, the plants would be able to discriminate between Backster's coming and going and that of another person less meaningful to them. It would be analogous to the reaction one might expect of a pet cat or dog, who knows his master.

The plants even discriminate between a thought that you do not really mean ("I'm going to get a match and burn a leaf") and a thought that is "for real."

On top of this discrimination capability, Backster also measured a discretionary capability. Plants were able to discern the difference between activities which, although they involved the well-being of the plant, were not important enough to be anxious about, and those that were.

You might say that humans have something to learn from plants with this capability. We worry about things that have only remote likelihood of affecting us. We need to acquire plants' ability to be discretionary with our anxieties and concerns and confine them to practical threats only.

AN ATTUNEMENT CAPABILITY IN PLANTS

With Backster being the only person taking care of his plants, he had an opportunity to test their reactions to his own emotions. Here again, no protocol was possible as the plants would easily "pick up" such contrivance. It had to be spontaneous – real life.

So Backster would hook up one of his plants to the polygraph, grab a notebook and a stopwatch, and do some errands around Times Square. Going down a subway entrance stairway and noting the exact time in his notebook; walking the length of the platform; asking a newsman, "Is this the latest edition?" and getting back an argumentative answer, "You don't believe me?"--all would be faithfully recorded on his laboratory charts as if the plant was with them.

What can you term such a result? Backster chooses the word attunement. Just as Gerald Langhorn was able to close his eyes, quiet his thoughts and sense what the sesame was "telling" him (he had the same success with sorghum, potatoes, beans and rice) which he called attunement, so Backster's plants were able to be attuned to Backster's thoughts and emotions.

Even on New Year's Eve, when thousands of people jammed Times Square, the plants zeroed in on one man – Backster – recording his walking as opposed to running, a different type of tracing, and his conversations, peaks and valleys depending on the emotions involved, right down to the time the New Year was signaled in.

Once he had to get his associate over to New Jersey where neighbors were having a surprise party for him and his wife on their anniversary. He hooked up the plants and took his notebook. Later checking the charts against his notebook, the plants had reacted to his running to catch a bus in the Port Authority, holding the bus door open, and even descending into the Lincoln Tunnel. When the neighbors yelled "Surprise!" the lines ran off the top of the paper, presumably because of the emotionality involved in the moment.

How do we humans digest the fact that plants have qualities similar to ourselves? How do we explain that plants can remember, that plants can feel your love, that plants have the ability to discriminate, to show discretion, to attune themselves to you in a crowd and at a distance?

It's enough to turn a vegetarian into a meateater. But, the vegetarian should meditate first on the possibility that plants perceive it as an honor to be eaten by man.

THE MEANING OF A "GREEN THUMB"

You and I might feel, well, this is all very interesting; let's see what develops; meanwhile, what else is new?

Backster did not have that luxury. He was immersed in the shock after shock of his discoveries. It turned him from an agnostic to a believer. But a believer in what?

Somehow, what emerged from his musings and ponderings was a persistent feeling that there existed a universal life force and that this life force was capable of a primary perception.

Way back in March of 1970, when the research was still in its initial stages, Backster was of that mind. Here is an edited transcription of remarks he made in a featured dinner talk at Wainright House, Rye, New York. This excerpt has to do with the green thumb concept.

"A person with a green thumb is a person who has accepted the idea that plants have a consciousness of their own. That's all there is to it. Despite poor care you may give it, that plant will still do wonders for you. Talk to it. Your words don't get through, but the mental imagery behind those words gets through. When you think about your plants, no matter where you are, they react to ft. It's as good as hovering over them and tending to them at home."

In order to accept the fact that plants have a consciousness of their own, Backster had to begin to perceive of consciousness filling all space. He had to believe in a oneness uniting all separateness.

He had to proclaim that we are not alone. Our thoughts are known by some pervading consciousness to which plants have access and, as his next research step would indicate, to which all living cells had access.

As he dared to say that evening at Wainright House, "There is no privacy. We cannot go up a dark alley and think we are getting away with something. We cannot abuse each other. We cannot harm the environment. We cannot commit a crime and think we are getting away with it.

"We can have no secrets."

Footnotes:

[1]*The Tao of Physics*, Fontana, London, 1975

[2]Perelanda, Ltd., Jeffersonton, Virginia

[3]September, "The Self-Reproducing Universe"

Chapter IV
Animal Organisms Caught In The Act Of Communicating

Tropical fig trees in Borneo depend on short-lived wasps for pollination. Each tree has its own fruiting timetable so that there are always some trees producing fruit at any given time of the year, thus keeping a supply of wasp pollinators on hand.

When this mystifying behavior was reported in the *New York Times* on Sunday, June 12, 1983[1] it quoted the reply of Jack C. Schultz, a Dartmouth College biologist who was asked whether this means that plants might possess consciousness or awareness of their environment. His reply was, "I would not go so far as to say that."

The article went on conservatively to state that scientists are beginning to develop a holistic approach toward the animal and plant kingdoms, now looking at a plant as a module and an animal as a unified organism.

They are in for a surprise. Backster's research points rather conclusively to each plant cell being such a module and each animal cell being a unified organism.

"If only we knew, Boss, what the stones and rain and flowers say. Maybe they call us – and we don't hear them. When will people's ears open, Boss?" So asks Zorba in Nikos Kazantzakis' *Zorba the Greek.*

"Not in our lifetime" is the answer to the question of when will we fully understand the complexities of the cell, given by Dr. Stanley Cohen, who shared the 1986 Nobel Prize in medicine. If he is correct, then he is likely commenting on his own life expectancy.

The Backster research is moving us quickly in the direction of that crucial understanding.   We could be on the edge of a stunning new concept that could benefit every living person on this planet.

FROM PLANT CELLS TO YOUR CELLS

Witness the following two apparently unrelated events:

1. A batch of 60 trees south of St. Louis are under study by Washington University researchers. For some reason every few years the trees produce an extraordinarily large crop of fruit, despite the fact that the flower crop is constant. How do the trees "collaborate" to produce simultaneous large crops?

2. A patient is under general anesthesia, totally "out" while surgery is being done. A tape is playing. Soothing suggestions are being made that they will recover more quickly and have fewer postoperative complications. That patient leaves the hospital one or two days earlier than other patients undergoing the same operation without the tape.

Do these two scenes have a common denominator?

To most conventional scientists, the answer is no.

To scientists who are able to integrate the Backster Effect into their belief systems, the answer is a qualified yes.

It is possible that the Backster Effect is behind the "collaboration" of the trees. Their roots are not in contact. Some are upwind of others and therefore out of chemical reach. But, there could be cell-to-cell communication, primary perception in action.

It is possible that the Backster Effect is behind the surgery patients' brain neurons being able to perceive auditory input even when the auditory organs on which they normally depend are deactivated. Primary perception is not a monopoly by plant cells. It is measurable in animal and human cells, too.

In order to bring the Backster Effect closer to your cells, we must first look at the research he has done with animal cells, and then currently with human cells.

In so doing, we will be treading pioneer ground – that is, in terms of classical physics. Nature does not toe the line which classical physics provides. This classical line provides for a world built of units like atoms. But Nature has a holistic character in the light of the quantum theory. So to understand Nature, we must leave classical physics behind. We cannot look at a plant, an animal, a human as a local automation. We must look at each and even the single cell as connected to a greater whole. We must examine the whole picture.

SCIENTISTS FIND BACKSTER EFFECT REPUGNANT AT PLANT AND CELLULAR LEVELS

Scientists cry "no!"

They cried "no!" when Backster's work was highlighted in "The Secret Life of Plants." They are still crying "no!", although the voices are a bit more muted.

Back in 1975, two plant physiologists and three animal physiologists met with Backster at a scientific symposium in New York. Their purpose for the two of them was to report on their unsuccessful attempts to replicate Backster's results and to offer their explanation of what was really happening in Backster's lab: his recording system was not properly shielded and so was receiving spurious signals.

Backster pointed out to these scientists that they were ignoring their own consciousness as a factor in the experiments – a factor that entered plants' primary perception – and that their synthetic laboratory protocol took the reality out of what they did, again, "known" to the plants. If there were spurious signals, they were the thoughts of these scientists signaling to the plants, "This is only an experiment."

The press attending the seminar seemed more supportive of Backster than of his challengers and were hungry for more details on his work with yogurt that yielded similar results pointing to a primary perception. One scientist present had tried and failed to repeat Backster's yogurt results, but the reporters had ears only for the positive.

Reported *Science News*,[2] "...the scientists left in various states of agitation, frustration, and embarrassment," with Backster still surrounded by animated reporters.

"Why did the scientific community take on Backster, anyway?" asked *Science News*. "What's wrong with people believing they can communicate with their plants?"

Backster's quoted comments were: "This phenomenon is real and it isn't going to go away. It's just as alive as any leaf out there and I am going to continue studying it and I hope other scientists will too."

He did. But they didn't.

EARLY EXPERIMENTS DISCLOSING PERCEPTION IN ANIMAL ORGANISMS SIMILAR TO PLANTS

When Backster was invited to speak before the staid, conservative American Association for the Advancement of Science in 1975, he was introduced as "the father of primary cell perception." To this introduction he responded, "The way you people have been receiving my research, I feel more like its unwed mother."

Because plants reacted to such signals as live shrimp dying in boiling water, blood cells dying in the coagulation of blood from an accidentally cut finger, and germs dying as they hit a urinal's antiseptic, it was natural that Backster turn his research from plants to animals.

Behind this change of emphasis was also his personal but firm belief that there was a "life force signal connecting all creation."

Working with unfertilized chicken eggs bought in a delicatessen near Times Square, Backster measured unexplained pulsations. The frequency of these electrical pulsations were the same as that of a chick embryo – 160 to 170 per minute. But there was no chick embryo inside the egg!

Backster automated the dropping of ten eggs into boiling water at staggered intervals. Another egg, not to be cooked, was monitored. This egg reacted violently as soon as the first egg entered the boiling water. However, as each of the other nine eggs were dropped, no reaction occurred.

Were the eggs in a state of shock? We might understand ourselves that way. It is a fallacy to interpret such reactions of simple organisms in complicated human terms, but there is not a shadow of doubt that a primary perception exists in chicken eggs having to do largely with survival.

This animal reaction jibes with plant reaction: Electrodes are attached to three different vegetables. An observer is asked to choose one of the vegetables to be dropped into boiling water. The instant that the vegetable is chosen in the mind of the observer, ups and downs on its chart straighten out indicating a turning off of its awareness, analogous to a faint. Variations continue on the other two veggie charts until the selected veggie is put into the boiling water. At that moment, the surviving veggies signal an increased agitation on their charts. (As a result of this, Backster suggests we notify both plant and animal food in advance that we are about to cook them, so they can protect themselves from "pain" with this coma-like state.)

Today Backster's laboratory in San Diego is not only profusely adorned by plants, but there are fish and eels in glass aquariums, samples of yogurt and other animal cell life in the refrigerator, with other live animals – such as a cat and a tortoise – roaming around the polygraph and electroencephalograph equipment, the microscopes and television monitoring equipment.

One factor in motivating Backster to move from plants to other forms of life, especially animal cells, was an unusual phenomenon.

When a plant reacted via the polygraph electrodes attached to its leaf, if the leaf was detached, the leaf itself reacted similarly. In fact, if an electrode sized piece of the leaf was tested, that small piece reacted as had the whole plant. One step further – and are you ready for this?– when the leaf was shredded and the particles spread on the electrode surfaces, the same reactions were recorded as if it were the whole plant.

Is this not reminiscent of the hologram? The matrix is exposed to an environment – say, a room. Then a laser beam is shone on to the matrix. The laser beam is tiny. It hits only a small fraction of the matrix. Yet, the whole room is outpictured in the resulting hologram. Just as it does not matter what leaf of the plant is chosen, or what tiny shreds of that leaf, it does not matter what part of the matrix is hit by the laser beam. The entire hologram of the room results.

This must make some scientists lie awake at night.

THE SWITCH FROM PLANTS TO ANIMALS

When Backster made his presentation to the Symposium at the 1975 annual meeting of the American Association for the Advancement of Science, he had already began to work with animal cells, even the human cells that have received since then the major thrust of his research. He barely mentioned this work at that time as he was getting enough flak on his plant work. It would only add fuel to the heated controversy he was generating.

Although not reported at the AAAS meeting in 1975, a Navy scientist, as early as 1973, was duplicating Backster's findings with considerable success. Eldon Byrd who, at that time, was an operations analyst with the Naval Ordinance Laboratory in Silver Springs, Maryland, attached the polygraph electrodes to plant leaves and observed reactions to thoughts of harming the plant and to such other stimuli as fire, water and stress. Byrd did not call these reactions "primary perception" but attributed the reactions to a voltage change in the cells due to a consciousness process.

This confirmation, bolstered by positive reports by several others and initial research with eggs and yogurt encouraged Backster to take the next logical step in his research – monitoring animal cells for clues to their having primary perception.

A new type of instrumentation seemed indicated. Up until then, Backster had been using the polygraph almost exclusively, in fact, mostly the Wheatstone Bridge and galvanometer features. Now Backster found that the electroencephalograph (EEG) was more useful. Used to monitor brain waves, the EEG gave him more flexibility in his measurements.

But other problems arose.

DIFFICULTY IN MONITORING ANIMAL CELLS

From the start, Backster chose bacterial cultures and some easy to obtain animal cells. But this was "child's play" with minimal portent compared to human cells. He saw more meaning for humankind if he could demonstrate primary perception in other cells of our bodies. So he switched quickly to human cells rather than wrestle with the problem of attaining animal cells and moved a step higher on the ladder of the evolution of matter. The human cells he chose were human spermatozoa, scrapings from the roof of the mouth and other human cell clusters.

These were maintained in an incubator under controlled temperatures as most of these types of human cells required a narrow temperature range for their survival. Even so, the survival time posed a problem. Also a problem was their extraction from the body.

After months of painstaking and frustrating attempts to settle on a dependable procedure, Backster decided to work almost exclusively with cells connected with the human immune system. Scientifically known as "in vitro leukocytes," these more commonly termed white cells showed some interesting initial monitoring results.

However, these cells circulating in the blood stream, whose job it is to fight infection and disease, were difficult to extract, needing continuing participation of medical doctors.

As if a higher intelligence were assisting Backster's work, he was alerted to a breakthrough that happened over a thousand miles away in Texas on a totally unrelated project, and a decade ago.

Dr. James M. Klinkhamer, then associate professor of Oral Research, Dental Branch, at the University of Texas, was researching new methods of diagnosing gingivitis in 1963. He was obtaining abundant amounts of white cells through a simple non-invasive procedure.

Backster quickly adopted this procedure and the collection of white cells could then be accomplished readily. He was then able to perfect a technology for electroding them so that they could be monitored with EEG-type instrumentation measuring their net electrical potential.

A number of exciting experiments then took place. Several have already been presented in previous chapters. Here is an example of another, this one done with human spermatozoa.

The donor was asked to be seated in a room about 40 feet from where his sperm cells placed in a beaker and monitored via silver wire electrodes attached to the electroencephalograph.

The read-out was almost a straight line, similar to what a person with an unsteady hand might draw (See figure 2). Backster held a capsule of amyl nitrite in his hand which the donor would inhale. Backster broke the capsule. At that very instant, before the vapor could be inhaled, the spermatozoa reacted suddenly and dramatically. Then as the gas was inhaled, the sharp swings of the pen on the read-out graph continued. In a few seconds they subsided.

Conclusion: A man's sperm cells are in touch with him long after they have been ejaculated and even at a distance.

Significance: Primary perception exists in human sperm

cells, a communication that can be considered of potential value in conception.

This summary – conclusion and significance – are the author's not necessarily the researchers, who from a professional standards point of view, need to be satisfied with "the facts, only the facts."

HUMAN MOUTH CELLS REACTING TO WAR, RAPE AND RAGE

By 1980, good things had begun to happen at the Backster Research Foundation in San Diego. Funds to expand the research were being donated; specialized equipment needed in the oral white cell work was received as a gift. And Stephen G. White joined in the work as a research associate.

Steve White first became acquainted with Backster's work when he was an undergraduate at San Diego State University. After receiving his Bachelor of Science degree he continued with his graduate studies and with the Backster Foundation research.

With the help of the new equipment and White, Backster was able to upgrade the records of his research by using split-screen video techniques. A black and white video camera is focused on the chart drive. A color video camera is focused on the donor. The two cameras then recorded on a single video tape both the chart tracing and the activities of the donor. To make the scientific protocol "cheese" more binding, a date-time generator displayed the session's time and date on the same video tape. Also, all of Backster's personnel vacated the laboratory.

This system allowed the researchers to play back any session as often as they needed in order to analyze stimulus-reaction correlations. And there were plenty!

One donor, whose white cells were placed in a test tube and the monitoring equipment activated, was asked to watch on his home television a program entitled "The World at War." It was no coincidence that the donor had served in the U.S. Navy and was stationed at Pearl Harbor during the Japanese attack.

There was a facial close-up of a naval gunner in action against enemy aircraft. The TV program, also being recorded in the laboratory, then showed the downing of an aircraft. Instantly the chart tracing showed a reaction by his mouth cells. (See Figure 3). As the television scene showed the enemy plane crashing into the

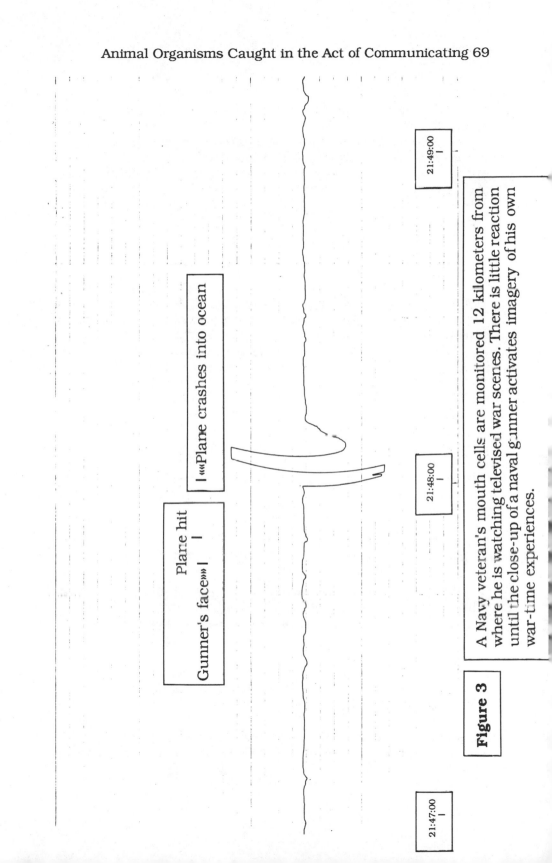

Figure 3

A Navy veteran's mouth cells are monitored 12 kilometers from where he is watching televised war scenes. There is little reaction until the close-up of a naval gunner activates imagery of his own war-time experiences.

sea, the chart tracing made a violent dip down and then an equivalently violent jump up.

Similar scenes that followed caused no repeat on the chart. Apparently, the only facial close-up had triggered the donor to image his own wartime experience. The donor later confirmed that he was indeed emotionally aroused at that point. His oral white cells were being monitored at a distance of some seven miles.

A female donor of oral white cells – she was 26 – was asked to watch an episode of "Hill Street Blues." She was only about a half mile from where her oral white cells were being monitored. As Backster's camera focused on the TV episode, an early scene depicted an undercover policewoman held in a car by a would-be rapist. An immediate reaction was recorded on the tracing of the white cells monitor. (See Figure 4).

In a post-session interview, she confirmed her emotional arousal at that scene as, when she was 19, she herself had been trapped in an automobile by a would-be rapist.

The same woman reacted again while watching that same television show, echoed by her oral white cells again a half a mile away. This time the television sequence showed a policeman pretending to shoot another policeman as part of a practical joke. The other policeman fell to the floor as if he had really been shot. The woman later expressed shocked indignation that such a scene was shown in a popular television program. The configuration of the chart read-out shows a typical reaction of human rage. (See Figure 5).

PLANNING FOR HUMAN REACTIONS

If the male donor was briefed in advance of the details of the film he was about to see and how what they were really looking for were his reactions to the aerial combat scenes, there would very likely be quite a different configuration on the split screen monitor of his mouth cells' reaction. Perhaps, no reaction at all.

Similarly, if the woman was given an orientation prior to the television show, it could have easily muted her mouth cells' reaction to either the would-be rapist scene or the mock shooting scene.

Yes, a war program was pre-planned for the veteran.

Yes, a program known for its violence was pre-planned for the woman.

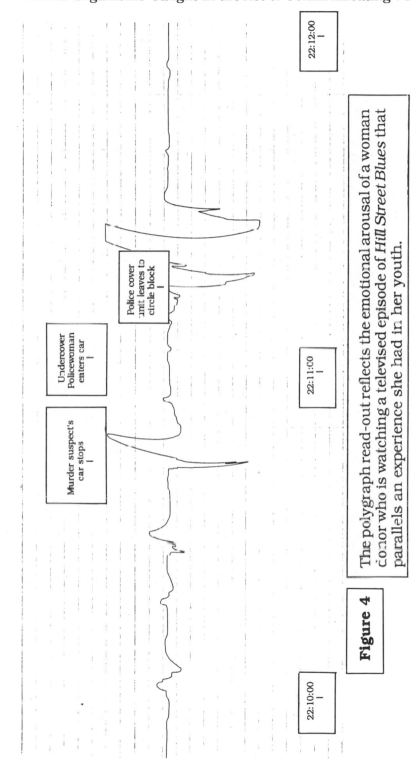

22:12:00

22:11:00

22:10:00

Figure 4

Police cover unit leaves to circle block

Undercover Policewoman enters car

Murder suspect's car stops

The polygraph read-out reflects the emotional arousal of a woman donor who is watching a televised episode of *Hill Street Blues* that parallels an experience she had in her youth.

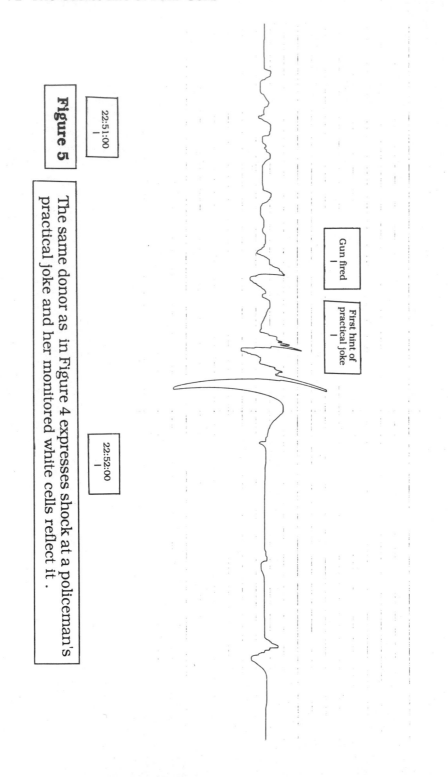

22:51:00

Gun fired

First hint of
practical joke

22:52:00

Figure 5

The same donor as in Figure 4 expresses shock at a policeman's practical joke and her monitored white cells reflect it .

It was helpful to Backster to have already catalogued by other disciplines the correlations between various psychological stimuli in humans and their corresponding electrophysiological reactions.

Since it is more important at this stage in his research to demonstrate cause-effect relationship than any subtle differentiation in the effects, there was no need to be selective in the types of emotions involved in the monitoring, only that there be definitive emotion.

Psychology and electrophysiology as well as some other discipline are in general agreement that certain stimuli cause electrical potential changes in humans. Fear and violence are certainly included.

In each of the three examples just given--and there are scores of others in the Backster files with the number growing monthly – the mouth cells' reactions were significant in their timeliness, amplitude and duration.

There is no doubt of the correlation of the time when the subjects experienced their emotional feelings and the time of the mouth cell "echo."

There is no doubt that the mouth cell reaction was indeed what it purported to be. The variation of amplitude on the chart was several times larger than the squiggles before and after.

There is no doubt that this reaction was valid and not the result of someone banging on the table, electrostatic discharge or other artifact, as its duration coincided largely with the time of the subject's maximum involvement.

Spontaneity was essential. You might use that old "saw" and stop a person's hiccups by scaring them. But, if you told them ahead of time what you were going to do, forget it. Let them sip some water.

This primary perception that is measured exists not only when it is measured, but it can be assumed to be an on-going phenomenon. So the perception is also there of the researcher's thoughts well in advance of the subject's participation.

Let's animate the situation:

Backster: See this dead frog. I'm going to cut open its abdomen while you watch. Let's see if your leukocytes being monitored on the other side of the room react.

Subject: Oh, I hate that. I used to turn my head away in high school lab. Do I have to watch?

Backster: Please do. At least once. It's in the interest of science.

Subject: Well, go ahead and get it over with.

Leukocyte (to other leukocytes in beaker): Hey, fellows, everything's quiet and copacetic. At ease.

Backster: There. The deed is done. Let's look at the read-out. (Looking at the chart.) Damn. Zilch.

A SCIENTIFIC LOOK AT THE PROCEDURE

If you were the subject, Backster would not have you submit to a scraping of your mouth using a standard tongue depressor. He won't ask you to say "Ah-h-h" as a physician using it in your mouth might. Instead, he would ask you to rinse your mouth with a specially prepared, slightly salty solution and to expectorate into a beaker.

He is actually implementing carefully regulated collection conditions which maximize white cell migration from the gums. Samples of this solution are then centrifuged, and transferred to a culture tube in preparation for electroding.

Let's have Cleve Backster and Steve White, his associate describe the next technical steps[3]:

The electroding technique, as refined during
thirty-six white cell monitoring sessions over the
past nine years, now prescribes the use of pure
gold electrodes. Two 60 mm lengths of gold wire,
diameter of 1 mm, are standard. One ml culture
tubes with outside dimensions of 6 X 50 mm were
utilized to contain the collected white cells.
It is important that the culture tube and the
top of the electrodes be firmly mounted. It
is also important that the electrodes, when
inserted in the culture tube, maintain
separation.

Two flexible wire leads were attached to
the top of the gold electrodes by means of small
firmly gripping alligator clips. Due to the
close proximity of the two gold electrodes,
care must be taken that the alligator clips do
not touch each other.

Net electrical potential activity of in
vitro white cells was monitored through the use
of EEG-type instrumentation.

Electrical signals were fed from the
electrode assembly, through a shielded cable, to
the biological preamplifier. The preamplifier
used was of a type suitable for EKG and EEG
recordings. It was set for EEG sensitivity.

Passband frequency settings were for a range of
0.2 Hz low and 50 Hz high.

The signal from the preamplifier was fed into
a recording amplifier which provided a sensitivity
control and a pen centering control. The output
of the recording amplifier actuated the high
frequency penmotor. The chart drive unit provided
a continuous recording capability producing
permanent ink tracings displayed on eight inch
(approximately 20 cm) wide chart paper moving
at the selected rate of six inches (approximately
15 cm) per minute.

This display provided a graphic read-out of
net electrical potential changes from the oral
leukocytes being monitored.

To insure the spontaneity so necessary for the observance of
primary perception, the researcher may pre-select the categories
of stimulus--sexual arousal, horror, etc., but a particular stimulus should not be presented at a specific time. To increase the
probability of an adequate reaction, the stimulus should evoke
emotions related to a negative effect on the well-being of the
donor. A stimulus that evokes a positive effect, that is, contributes to the well-being of the donor, does not generally produce an
effect easily observable.

Does that give us a clue to the nature of primary perception?
It relates to the protection of life.

Often Backster's skills as a former CIA interrogator and also
with his polygraph interviews are helpful in selecting suitable

general categories for the stimulus. He holds a pre-session consultation with the subject which gives him the information he needs about a subject's background and sensitivities.

Later, when the reactions of the mouth cells are being assessed, the same criteria can be used as are used when the sensors are applied directly to the subject's body and the psychophysiological tracings evaluated.

This additional correlation between the body and the body's cells at a distance certainly adds to the awesomeness of the Backster Effect.

ELECTRICAL AND MAGNETIC EFFECTS ON LIVING ORGANISMS

Electrical instruments which pick up electrical changes in the human body are now in common usage. Skin galvanic reactors measure relaxation responses by detecting changes in the electrical properties of the skin. The EEG measures electrical wave frequency output of the brain. Electrocardiograms (EKG) measure the heart's functioning by its tiny electrical impulses.

Still, we know little today about the part that electricity and electromagnetism play in living organisms.

In the 18th century, a German physician named Frederick Anton Mesmer presented to the medical faculty of the University of Vienna a paper entitled "The Influence of the Stars and Planets as Curative Powers." The sun, moon and stars, he said, affected humans through a force which could also be derived from a magnet. He called this force "animal magnetism."

At the same time, a Jesuit priest with the unlikely name of Father Hell was obtaining dramatic cures by applying magnetized steel plates to the patient's body.

Mesmer worked for a while with Father Hell, but then began to work independently using other magnetized objects.

Soon popular and professional journals were reporting vivid accounts of how Mesmer's magnets were curing apparently hopeless cases. Thousands of invalids poured into Vienna each week as Mesmerism became a European byword.

Can you foretell what happened next?

Right: The inevitable backlash by vested interests. His colleagues maintained a steady attack to discredit him. Eventually Mesmer was forced to flee from Vienna to Paris. He returned years later to Vienna where he died a pauper, remembered not for cures but for quackery.

But there was a revival of the use of metals, magnets and electricity in France in the mid-19th century. A physician named Victor Burq found that copper and other metals tended to restore sight, hearing and feeling in hysterics. He influenced the noted neurologist Jean-Martin Charcot who had confirmed his findings. By the late 1880's, French physicians were using magnets to produce anesthesia and changes in circulation.

With the return of Sino-American relations, an upsurge of interest has occurred in acupuncture, but here, too, the prejudice against electrical approaches to healing by the American medical fraternity is keeping acupuncture in the professional deep freeze.

The only clear-cut electrical therapy that is in widespread use is shock therapy for the mentally ill. But a new application has just opened medical eyes.

It would still be largely unknown, as it is currently receiving the Mesmer treatment, had it not been for the reporting skills of television's ABC. Their program called "20/20" aired a fascinating sequence on Oct. 21, 1988 (Honolulu date) featuring the work of Dr. Bjorn Nordenstrom a Swedish specialist in diagnostic radiology connected with the Karolinsku Institute in Stockholm.

Dr. Nordenstrom has successfully used electrical currents to cure cancerous lung tumors. He applies electrodes so that the current goes through the walls of blood vessels and capillaries and hence through the tumor. Three of his "terminal" patients treated in 1978 are still alive today.

Because the theory is so complex and its applications so precise, it would not be possible to present the approach to the medical profession via the usual terse papers. So he wrote a book. If you really want to affront vested interests, write a book. Had it not been at least partly for the program "20/20", Dr. Nordenstrom's work would have been effectively trampled on. Instead, it is now catching fire with a number of more daring therapists. We will hear more about that work.

Backster has been written about considerably, but his own writings have been confined largely to professional papers.

Should the current revival of interest in the magnetic and electrical aspect of life be more than fleeting, it could well throw some light on the nature of primary perception in plants and animal cells.

Electrotherapy has been used somewhat successfully in pain control and in the healing of stubborn bone fractures. Current has been used to regenerate spinal nerves in animals. An Indian researcher has reversed rabies paralysis in animals through the application of a direct current.

ADVERSE EFFECT OF ELECTRICAL POWER LINES

The fact that electrical and magnetic fields can also have adverse effects on animal and human life strengthens the case for further study of these fields as bearing on primary perception.

It has been found that electrical fields from power lines in the United States which at 60 Hz (cycles per second) affected the normal pineal gland rhythms in rats; that animals exposed to a 50 Hz drank and ate less; that changes in the magnetic field around the human scalp could touch off migraine headaches.

Many of our modern day devices put out magnetic and electromagnetic fields. Examples are microwave ovens, hairdriers, and loudspeakers.

At the present writing a controversy is raging on the island of Oahu in Hawaii where the route of a proposed highway and tunnel would be forced by the mountain configuration to pass in close proximity to a Coast Guard radio installation with a high radiant energy, so high it causes shocks to pedestrians and would have similar effects on cars and their occupants, even interfering with heart pace-makers.

The Health Effects Laboratory of the Environmental Protection Agency is currently studying the effects of exposure to electrical fields found in the average home. Does this exposure cause changes or affect growth? So far the answer is yes at least as far as chickens are concerned. Electrical fields of normal intensity in homes affected their developing nervous systems.

Let's end this review on a positive note.

As early as 1971, experiments were being performed on grains of wheat planted in sand and water and then exposed to various types of extremely low frequency (E.L.F.) electrical signals. Their growth averaged 23% greater than wheat grains not so exposed. E.L.F. frequencies are not the 50 and 60 Hz put out by ambient power lines but the 10 Hz put out by humans. That is the frequency of the alpha waves recorded by the EEG equipment.

In those days, an E.L.F. phenomenon was noticed in the ionosphere. Alpha waves similar to those recorded by the EEG when attached to the human head were measured high in the atmosphere. "Probably due to thunderstorms" was the explanation. But a billion human brains pulsating at that frequency where the wavelength approximates the circumference of the earth seems a more likely explanation.

If this is so, we are all part of an electrical field or continuum, the study of which might lead humankind to some revolutionary approaches to progress in health and longevity.

Brain/Mind Bulletin[4] recently devoted almost an entire issue to current research into magnetic and electromagnetic effects on living systems. In reporting on the work of Ross Adey of the Veteran's Neurobiology Research Group which showed that these fields increased enzyme activity associated with both normal and malignant growth, he was quoted as predicting that they "betoken a biological revolution of vast proportions that will touch every basic area of cellular biology, from (embryonic development) to aging and cancer."

CONGRESS EXPRESSES INTEREST IN BACKSTER'S CELLULAR COMMUNICATIONS

On June 4 and 5, 1974, hearings were held before a subcommittee of the committee on Government Operations in the House of Representatives concerning the use of polygraphs and similar devices by federal agencies.

After Backster was questioned an hour on skills needed to operate the polygraph, the questioning turned to his experimentation with plants. Here is an excerpt from those hearings:

Mr. Cornish: Mr. Chairman?

Mr. Moorhead: Mr. Cornish?

Mr. Cornish: Do I understand that you are doing some sort of experimentation with plants?

Mr. Backster: Your understanding is correct.The thing I did, and it was 8 years ago, was attach the electronic or galvanic skin response section of the polygraph to a plant leaf. This led to, as a matter of fact, 8 years of exploration where we found that we can use a patch of the plant leaf, or we can grind the leaf up and test the cellular response. From this we converted to the use of the electroencephalograph to take biological readings. At the present, we are over into the animal life field, at cellular level.

I suspect that we are going to be able to show that cells, taken from the human body and put in one incubator, and additional cells taken from the same source and put in another incubator, will show communication capability from one part of the sample to the other. This ties to something which I think could be important in the field of immunology.

Since you brought this up, so far as my history of involvement in this is concerned, I got quite a bit of kidding initially. After the initial observation, I immediately estimated whether it would be beneficial to pursue the matter and then decided to put it before the scientific and academic communities.

I have here, which I would like to submit to the subcommittee, a partial list of lectures to the scientific and academic communities over a period of 8 years. All of these relate to this subject. I think the amount of interest and the frequency of the invitations to participate by giving symposiums, seminars, and so on, will perhaps indicate their interest.

If I might submit this?

Mr. Moorhead: Yes; the committee would be glad to receive that.

At this point Backster submitted a list of his lectures from 1969 to 1974 which numbered over 30 and included universities and research societies. Among these were NASA, M.I.T., American Association for Humanistic Psychology, and American Academy of Psychotherapists.

The questioning continued.

Mr. Cornish: The reason I bring this subject up is not to go into detail, but there is a great deal of interest in so-called communication with plants and that sort of thing these days. Can you tell me whether you actually attach a polygraph to a plant?

Mr. Backster: No, I used the galvanic skin response electrodes only, which enabled me to stumble upon the idea that there was electrical activity at the cellular level. I then converted to the use of the electroencephalograph. I think there has been a fair amount of interest – in fact, even the housewives sort of think the research is pertinent to some of the things that they have been thinking right along.

But I had second thoughts initially, I think, on this involvement. It took a little courage of my convictions to pursue it. Certainly my reputation within the polygraph field was at stake.

I think by looking at this list you can see the representative interest current in the scientific and academic communities.

HOW FAST DOES CELLULAR COMMUNICATION TRAVEL?

Is biocommunication taking place at some point in the electromagnetic wavelength spectrum and must it go from here to there?

Or, is it rather an instantaneous perception by a field of intelligence that permeates all space?

While conventional scientists bicker about the existence of the phenomenon, more adventuresome scientists are ready to accept the phenomenon and proceed further by searching out the answer to the question, "What is the nature of this beast?"

The element of time could determine which of these two alternatives were closest to the truth.

Yes, research into this biocommunication phenomenon could lead to new avenues of knowledge in the fields of genetics, the healing process, immunology and the mind-body connection.

But, research into the signal itself – especially the propagation factor--could provide valuable insight into new kinds of communication; or possibly a new form of energy, or even that universal field of intelligence that is beginning to tantalize those scientists at other frontiers which we will discuss later.

Comments Backster on these prospects in the conclusions of his Biocommunications Capability report cited earlier in this chapter:

"At present, the biocommunication under discussion involves a signal about which there is still inadequate information. Scientific method would seem to prescribe exploration relating to the basic nature of this phenomenon, its fundamental characteristics, its geographical limits, its mode of transmission, its susceptibility to shielding, its influence on matter, its information retention capabilities, its stimuli discrimination capabilities, etc.

"Even within this limitation, it is possible to perform meaningful research related to the susceptibility to shielding and distance limitations. The introduction of cryogenic technology into the methodology could allow monitoring of in vitro white blood cells at considerable earth distances from their donor. Should there be meaningful observations at such distances, the same technology, with the addition of telemetry, would be justifiable as part of a space probe to determine possible attenuation effect and time consumption of the signal."

Are you ready to send your mouth cells into space?

Footnotes:

[1]"The Plant Biologists Turn Over a New Leaf" by Bayard Webster

[2]Volume 107, February 8, 1975

[3]*Biocommunications Capability: Human Donors and in Vitro Leukocytes*, reprinted with permission, International Journal of Biosocial Research, Volume 7 (2): 132-146, 1985

[4]Volume 4, No. 1, October, 1988, P.O. Box 42211, Los Angeles, CA 90042

Chapter V

Primary Perception
Human To Human

What about you and I? Are our cells perceiving our thoughts? Are my cells perceiving yours, or yours mine? And if the answer is "yes," what does that mean to you and me?

To place Backster's work in proper perspective regarding the significance relative to these answers, it is of value to know that whisperings of the phenomenon can be found in the literature of the start of this century and even as the squiggles and jerks of the EEG equipment continue in San Diego today, parallel work is going on elsewhere in the world.

It is all going to come together one day. The impact on your life and mine will be stunning. It will be positive. New knowledge, properly applied, has always meant new levels of life's enjoyment for humankind. The secret life of your cells, bared for two-way communications between you and them, promises added years to your life and life to your years.

INTELLIGENCE IN CELLS NOTED DECADES AGO

Where there is smoke there is fire.
Cells have been "smoking" for decades.

Here are some references to the signs of human-like intelligence in cells spotted in various publications going back over 50 years.

In 1913 *Scientific American* published an article by S.L. Bastin entitled "Can Plants Feel Pain?" in which he says,

"It is now generally recognized that there is no essential difference between the evidences of life in the plant and in the animal...Small wonder then that Dr. Francis Darwin and others should discuss the question of plant consciousness and seek for signs of memory in the vegetable being.[1]"

He was published in the same magazine the following year, asking "Have Plants An Unknown Sense?" Here he asserts,

"...plants appear to have a special sense...[and] we now know that plants are able to feel objects at a distance...as if they were aware of the presence of a certain thing, even though they may not be in contact at all.[2]"

The electrical properties of trees, not measured anywhere near as precisely as Backster measured that of his plants, was nevertheless reported by Harold S. Burr in countless published articles between 1935 and 1960 including such publishers as the *Proceeds of the National Academy of Science, Growth,* and *Yale Journal of Biology and Medicine.*

You will get his drift from just the titles:

"Electrical Characteristics of Living Systems"

"The Electro-Dynamic Theory of Life"

"Bio-Electric Potential Gradients in the Chick"

"An Electro-Metric Study of Mimosa"

"Response of the Slime Mold to Electric Stimulus"

"Effects of a Severe Storm on the Electrical Properties of a Tree and the Earth"

Let's examine one of Burr's contentions:

"...since it has been adequately demonstrated that a living organism, the tree, is an electrical system exhibiting all the properties of an electrical field, one may reasonably expect that changes in the electric environment will show some interrelationship with the field properties of the tree...Sharp spikes appear in the record during the storm...they are evidence of a very profound change in the earth and atmospheric electricity."

A neuroanatomist, Burr's main thrust was to study the energy fields around plants and animals. His most dramatic discovery was that young salamanders had an energy field shaped like the adult salamander. He traced this back and found it even in the unfertilized egg. He also found that a plant sprout had the same electrical field as the adult plant.

In 1969, F.L. Kuntz, writing in *Main Currents in Modern Thoughts*, was one of the first to give a positive assessment of the philosophical implications of the early Backster research.

From then on, we see a cavalcade of articles in both the scientific and popular literature exploring the evidence of cell communication. Again, just citing typical titles to illustrate the thinking:

"Short-term Memory in Plants"
"Electrical Coupling Between Cells of Higher Plants"
"Electropotentials of Plant Cells"
"The Magnetic Memory of the Virus"
"Memory and Perception Mechanisms in Bacteria"

Backster never really smelled this smoke before that night of February 2, 1966. It was natural curiosity about the rate that water rose from root to leaf in a plant that made him attach the Wheatstone bridge circuitry. He had never heard of Bastin or Burr or Kuntz.

He smelled more than smoke after that. He conscientiously researched most of the literature on the subject, and proceeded to blaze his own research trails.

PRIMARY PERCEPTION:
THE HUMAN CONNECTION

We have traced Backster's research trails from plants, to animals and now to humans.

Just as this required backtracking to his early research days and then catching up to the present to stand shoulder to shoulder with him as he caught human cells in the act of perceiving human thought, it now requires us to move on past him to case the area and see where the trail leads.

This then shifts from Backster's research to the author's own research. This research is in two categories: direct and indirect.

The direct research involves years of working with metaphysics, hypnosis and self-hypnosis, psychotronics (the study of the energy of consciousness) and the effects of activating the brain's right hemisphere through meditation techniques and the Silva Method.

The indirect research involves decades of exposure to the work of others in the field of holistic health, theosophy, intuitive functioning, and paranormal phenomena.

Stand shoulder to shoulder with the author now to better understand his direct and indirect research activities. First the direct.

A score of Silva Method graduates are seated comfortably in a Honolulu living room. It is evening. Trade winds rustle the palm trees outside, the only sounds heard as the group does some collective deep breathing with eyes closed. The author then leads them in a countdown exercise which helps to slow down their brain wave rhythm while at the same time activating the right brain. He then instructs them as follows:

"Please picture Roslyn Brown. She is 34 and lives in Kuala Lumpur, Malaysia. She has a chronic cough. She is not a smoker. Please detect the problem and correct it."

While the group searches for the problem in their imagination, the author is doing likewise. This search involves scanning the body – this can be done from both an exterior and interior viewpoint – and asking to "see" the abnormality. Perhaps the attention is drawn to the lungs where some black spots are noticed. If so, then the black spots are erased, or rubbed out, or painted over, anything which then permits the imagined picture of the lungs to be perfect, free of the abnormality.

The dynamic meditation session is ended and the graduates might compare notes.

"I saw fluid in the lungs so I removed it with a siphon."

"There was an inflammation in the trachea. I applied a soothing salve."

"I received the impression of foreign matter in the lungs. I vacuumed it out."

There might be agreement among half of those present on one of the possibilities and the others divided among several other possibilities. But the final picture held in the minds of all present was identical: Roslyn Brown with a beautiful, healthy respiration system.

A week later, a letter arrives from Roslyn Brown in Malaysia, "My cough is gone."

Coincidence? Unexplained remission? Responding to previously taken medication? What does it matter what cause-effect relationship the logical left brain hemisphere demands. Action at a distance has taken place again and again with the amount of "miracles" so huge that there are now over eight million graduates of the Silva Method around the world and medical science has tentatively adopted one of its applications and calls it psychoneuroimmunology.

This is the patient "talking" to his own blood cells. But we can talk to other people's cells, too.

The human connection is there. Where? Everywhere.

TO WHAT DOES THE HUMAN CONNECTION CONNECT?

As to indirect research, the author has regularly reviewed such popular magazines as *Fate* and *New Realities* to such more technical periodicals as *Brain/Mind Bulletin* and *Science*. Where reports pique his curiosity, additional information is frequently obtained as a follow-up. Wherever possible he has met with direct researchers to probe into the significance and potentiality of their work.

Just as this led to familiarity with the Backster Effect, so is it currently leading to familiarity with other professional investigations which, although along different trails than Backster's, are breakthroughs just as dramatic.

As the data from the author's direct and indirect research is accumulated in his 30 billion component computer, called the brain, the cybernetic effect causes views to emerge that go beyond the input data.

As we walk shoulder to shoulder through the pages ahead, we will begin to see possibilities for our understanding and use of the human cell's secret ability to know our thoughts and to react to these thoughts.

Even if we merely allow that psychoneuroimmunology is but part of the whole mind/body connection; we have the key to "talking" ourselves well. It turns out that this is so simple a pre-kindergartner can do it. The ultimate finding is still short of the ultimate truth.

But it does point to the validity of all the metaphysical, philosophical, theological, and theosophical literature over the ages that points to a non-physical basis to the physical world.

"Non-physical" is a non-word. Science does not have a word for the causal realm because it delves only into the effect realm. So we must use such words as "energy" or "spiritual." The author will be using these two words interchangeably.

Whichever word is used, it denotes not a nothingness, but a somethingness. This somethingness has something to do with the primal energy of the material universe crystallizing into atoms.

When these atoms combine into molecules and cells, this somethingness has something to do with the human's ability to be in touch with other humans anywhere.

The ultimate human connection is to this somethingness. We'll be getting better acquainted with it as we move along the trails currently being blazed.

Get ready to meet a part of you which you know very little about, if anything at all. Consider the body which you know to be yourself as only a part of you – you the effect.

Here comes you the cause.

A POSSIBLE RELATIONSHIP
BETWEEN THE BENEFITS OF POSITIVE THINKING
AND THE BACKSTER EFFECT

Our present understanding of the human being is still largely oriented to Newtonian physics. Even though this paradigm was strikingly extended by Einstein, no movement in the Einsteinian direction has yet taken place by our common understanding.

Nor has there been any change in the understanding of the human body by the medical profession. The Newtonian block-by-block structure of the human being is still in vogue. Physicians are balking at adopting the Einsteinian concept of the human being which is as interpenetrating, interactive fields of energy.

Doctors see the human body as the only dimension of being. Energy fields? What cannot be examined by surgical dissection just is not there, Einstein notwithstanding.

Are there no young Turks who will dare to break out of this rigid, antiquated mold? Not very many. One of the most successful, Carl Simonton, M.D., lost his practice. Others need to be hassled a lot less than Simonton to give up their beliefs and toe the allopathic line – too much of an investment to want to see go down the drain, too rosy a future to want to see it muddied up.

"I'll give up my insight into the human being as dependent on energy system for health and revert to the concept of bodies being just flesh and bones. I've got to feed my family."

Bernie Siegel, M.D., may have provided the professional encouragement that will give physicians more daring to take that one step beyond. A member of the Yale University faculty and a practicing surgeon in New Haven, Connecticut, Dr. Siegel became president of the young American Holistic Medical Association in 1988.

That was probably the same year that his book, *Love, Medicine and Miracles* hit a million copy sale. In it he relates case after case of where patients who change from an attitude of hopelessness to one of hopefulness reversed the course of their disease, even cancer.

What is hope?   Let's put it under a microscope for all Newtonian physicians to see. Hope is a thought. It is a thought that concerns the life of your cells. Are they interested in that thought? You better believe it. Can they perceive that thought? Well, if your mouth cells can perceive that you are looking at a girlie magazine, even when those mouth cells are a distance from your body, certainly your lung cells, fighting to win the battle over cancer, can perceive the pat on the back that your positive thoughts of hope bring to them.

Dr. Siegel sees positive thinking in patients as a number one priority. From the misfortune you suffer, you must wring out good. This change in the polarity of consciousness gets to the body's cells and causes a change in health from bad to good.

How does the positivity of thoughts get perceived by the cells of the body?

Is it telepathy?

Extra-sensory perception?

Psychic ability?

A field of intelligence (such as Dr. Rupert Sheldrake's morpho-genetic field)?

Primary perception?

And if it fits into any of these poorly defined pockets, how about a healthy explanation of that pocket? It is energy which all of them undoubtedly are but what kind of energy?

There may be a dozen more possible "pockets," but even these, because they go beyond the present paradigms of Newtonian physics and would have to be explained by Einsteinian ap-proaches, will sound implausible, mystic, or "far out." Exit the very people whose interest must be harnessed in order to harness the mysterious energy.

A mental healer "sees" a person's lungs perfect miles away and immediately the lungs respond.

Live shrimp are dropped into boiling water and a plant at the other end of the laboratory responds.

A donor sees violence on television and his mouth cells, captured in a receptacle miles away, respond.

A woman relaxes and visualizes her husband. She pleads mentally for him to phone her. He responds.

All four instances are the communication of intelligence. All four instances involve space between sender and receiver.

All four instances bypass the known senses. All four instances make classical scientists uneasy.

Maybe this is because they are afraid of evidence for there being a God. And maybe they're right. But meanwhile, they better bone up on the Einsteinian and quantum implications.

HOW HUMAN BRAIN NEURONS CAN CONTACT OTHER HUMAN BRAIN NEURONS MILES AWAY

Two quantum physicists at Stanford Research Institute (SRI) in Palo Alto, California, have worked for more than five years on a successful research project which they call "Remote Viewing." The U.S. government is interested for its military potential.

If you participated, you would be sealed into a room with one or more observers. A remote location is selected randomly and a second experimenter visits that location which could be hundreds of miles away.

You are not told anything about the randomly selected site. But you are asked to describe it verbally and/or by sketch.

Whether you volunteered for this experiment because you were passing by, or because you are an army general, you are likely to succeed. Just about every description has resulted in "hits" that go beyond the possibility of chance.

A building is accurately described right down to the arch or the dome. A park is sketched and everything – even the fountain – is in its proper place. A harbor and pier are correct.

Some people are better than others. These are usually individuals who have already demonstrated psychic ability. Ingo Swann, a New York artist and psychic, was not only able to describe distant sites accurately but was able also to describe the weather conditions there at that time. Harold Sherman and Ingo Swann, who had conducted similar experiments before with polar explorers, demonstrated their remote viewing by describing conditions on Mercury and Jupiter that were later confirmed by telemetry data from NASA's satellite missions.

In the latter case, there were no human brain neurons for the psychic to tap at the other end. In many of SRI's randomly chosen sites, this was also true. So, whatever the nature of this perception, it does not have to depend on a neuron-to-neuron connection. It is "of itself;" and so it can be properly called primary perception.

This one way perception adds a new dimension to the Backster Effect. Backster initiates an event. The event triggers a response at a distance. Here, however, there is only the response of the brain neurons to the desire.

"What does the site look like that the computer has randomly selected?" The question is asked mentally; the answer comes mentally. It is as if the human mind has access to the whole universe. All it has to do is ask!

"Wait a minute," a voice over my shoulder insists, "Aren't you shoveling that stuff a little hard?"

I look around. It is the voice of all those people who have not had time to read the half million papers published each year in brain science alone. Even if they were conversant with Jung's collective unconscious, Sheldrake's morphogenetic field, Rhine's ESP, Russell's Global Brain, and the Silva Mind Control Method, it would be a good beginning.

It would be the alchemy that transforms what is apparently stable matter into the reality of an energy world.

Perhaps the most alchemy takes place when one studies the holographic theory of the universe proposed simultaneously by American surgeon Karl Pribram and Nobel prize-winning British physicist David Bohm, neither knowing about the other's work until their respective papers were published. This unlikely synchronicity is like a universal echo confirming their mutual theory, which sees the universe as connected.

Is primary perception another echo of this connection?

SUBJECTIVE COMMUNICATION-- A UNIVERSAL "AT&T?"

The SRI work involving another human on the distant site presumably enables the sequestered "observer" to tap into the brain neurons of this person who is a direct viewer. So the remote viewer is helped by the direct viewer.

This relationship then becomes a two-way "conversation"

below the level of consciousness (or above it). The direct viewer does not sense that his or her brain is being "tapped."

The remote viewer does not sense a reaching but merely gets views in his or her imagination which feel like fantasizing or guessing.

This is known as subjective communication. It is a successfully used mental functioning by people trained with the Silva Mind Control Method.

Here is how it works and a sampling of the ways in which it has been successfully used.

Silva Method trainees learn to slow their brain waves to half the normal awake frequency in the first few hours of the four-day training. This is called the alpha level. At the alpha level, the right hemisphere of the brain becomes more active. Thinking becomes bicameral.

Thousands of recent brain science papers have touched on right brain functioning. We will get to the meat of them later, but for now let us just say that the evidence points to the left brain being devoted to the physical world and the right brain being devoted to the non-physical world. So the left brain is objective, the right brain is subjective.

Left brain – objective – communication involves our voices, our ears, our eyes, and other physical amplifiers and/or media.

Right brain – subjective – communication involves the mind's unexplained abilities demonstrated in such phenomena as remote viewing.

When you go to the alpha level and mentally picture a person, your brain neurons are "in touch" with that person. You can "talk" to that person without speaking a single word!

That's the good news.

Now the bad news.

You have to love that person. So, if you are beginning to think about reaming out your boss, forget it. Putting your spouse down is not going to get through either. Nor is mentally spanking a child.

These are left brain modalities.   The left brain thrives on polarity. So much of our objective communication is polarized. I'm right. You're wrong. But when it goes in one ear and out the other, then subjective communication is indicated,--and that means no polarity.

Loving the recipient of your subjective conversation brings about two changes in the visual left brain approach.

1. You feel a togetherness and equality with the recipient.
2. You do not think in terms of *who* is right, but rather *what* is right for the both of you.

Suppose you have a three-year-old boy who is wetting the bed. The more you talk to him about it, the wetter the bed seems to get. So you can decide to use subjective communication. You relax physically and mentally.

"You lousy brat. Next time you wet your bed I'll push your face in it!"

Sorry. You still have a bedwetter in the house.

How about this instead.

"Darling, if you have to go, get up and do it in the toilet. You'll sleep better in a dry bed and I'll have less work to do."

Congratulations! It worked.

Follow the rules and it always works. You never get a wrong number. But don't take all the credit yourself. Give some to whatever it is in space that makes primary perception in general and subjective communication in particular work - the universal communication media that, for the time being, must go nameless.

SOME PRACTICAL USES FOR YOUR CELLS' SECRET ABILITY TO SEND AND RECEIVE MESSAGES

The author's own personal experiences are replete with cases where his subjective communications were eminently success-ful--as well as those that failed.

It is more difficult to understand the successes than to explain the failures.

Subjective communication fails when any one of the following conditions are present:

1. You did not expect it to be successful.
2. You were not physically relaxed.
3. You were not mentally relaxed.
4. You neglected to image the recipient.
5. You did not sincerely feel rapport or love.
6. You sought a solution for yourself that either created a problem or entailed no advantage to the recipient.

But when it works, why in the world does it work?

A daughter gives up her resentment over a financial incident.

A group of neighbors, antagonistic toward lecturing activities, cease their obstructionism.

A biased judge agrees to let a colleague settle the case.

A husband, who has demanded abstention in their married life in the interests of higher consciousness, after six months of no sex from him and 30 seconds of subjective communication from her, takes his wife to bed.

What is happening?

What is the possible parallel with primary perception?

What are the possibilities for human betterment?

At the present writing, the author's first novel is seeking a publisher. In it the hero uses subjective communication to win the heroine, to engineer the release of hostages in a foreign land, to detect the true motivation behind certain diplomatic maneuvers, to induce iron countries to seek their freedom, to bring about one world.

The novel will seem strange to many editors. But after all, is truth not even stranger than fiction?

The story is one person's view of the path that research into primary perception in its many facets can lead.

With that view comes a surge of respect of love from the author for all the brave right brain researchers in this left brain world.

A tip of the hat to Dr. Marcel Vogel, an IBM chemist, when he was one of the first to successfully replicate Backster's work with plants; and to Dr. Harold Puthoff, one of the driving forces behind SRI's Remote Viewing work and a skilled laser physicist.

Some key people who moved the frontier of physics forward in the past couple of decades so that it could begin to include such phenomena as primary perception are Andrija Puharich, M.D., a neurophysiologist of Ossining, New York; Christopher Hills, head of University of the Trees in Boulder Creek, California; Richard Gerber, M.D., author of *Vibrational Medicine*; James Beal, a NASA physicist; Brendan O'Regan, a brain chemist at the Design Science Institute; and William Tiller of Stanford University. Apologies to the many not mentioned.

The scientists who are casualties because they got stepped on too early for their careers to survive will never be known. Just the way that whistleblowers are relegated to oblivion by vested interests; so have many brilliant young scientists been forced by economic reality to swallow their beliefs, and to conform.

Yes, a tip of the hat to the scientists who dared to persevere. Bared heads for the others.

YOUR CELLS HAVE A
CONSCIOUSNESS OF THEIR OWN

Our brain neurons can contact brain neurons belonging to another person.

We used to confine that notion to the weird occasions when a mother awoke from a dream and knew her daughter was in an accident. A long distance call confirmed it.

But now we have the ability under control with remote viewing and subjective communication. We can use "mind-speak" person-to-person.

Certainly that is good. But is it all the good there is?

No. It is only the beginning.

You can "talk" to your body cells. Your body cells can "talk" to you. You can "talk" to somebody else's body cells. And they can "reply."

These discoveries appear to our logical mind to be impossible. But since they are not only possible and indeed they are fact, then there needs to be a change of mind.

Not everybody is ready, willing and able to change their mind, especially professionals who have spent years and dollars in attaining their present mind state.

In his book "Global Mind Change," Dr. Willis Harmon, the current president of the Institute for Noetic Sciences, states, "We are already well into the mind change. It is altering the way we interpret science; it is drastically modifying our concepts of health care; it is revolutionizing our concepts of education; it is causing major changes in the world of business and finance; it is in the process of delegitimating war..."

Dr. Harmon delineates three metaphysical perspectives which he calls M-1, M-2, and M-3.

M-1 is *materialistic monism* which says that matter gives rise to mind.

M-2 is *dualism* which says there is matter and there is also mind.

M-3 is *transcendental monism* which says that mind gives rise to matter.

The change in mind is underway from M-1 to M-3, an understanding of the universe which is far more comfortable in the western mind today than it was a generation ago.

In science, it is seen in the concepts of anti-matter, of action at a distance, of space permeated by fields of intelligence.

In health care, it is seen in the concepts of the mind affecting the body.

In education, it is exemplified by the recommendation made at the annual meeting of the American Educational Research Association that schools include the Silva Method in curricula.

In business, at this writing, there is an on-going process among business schools and corporations that there is a virtue in being virtuous. Harvard Business School now has a mandatory course in ethics and General Dynamics has established a vice presidency for ethics.

In international relations, peace is breaking out and armaments are being disarmed.

A change of mind. A change in consciousness. On a global level. Are we all one? Does consciousness permeate all space?

And does every living cell – plant, animal, human – share that consciousness?

MIND-SPEAK: HOW TO COMMUNICATE SUBJECTIVELY WITH OUR OWN BODY CELLS

Bernie Siegel, M.D. tells how he put on the bulletin board of the Yale New Haven Hospital's doctors lounge, a statistically valid double-blind study by a San Francisco cardiologist on the benefits of prayer in reducing postmyocardial infarction (heart attack) complications. A day later, somebody had written "bullshit" across it.

In 1975, the author attended the Second World Psychotronic Conference in Monte Carlo. A team of Czech physicians reported on a study which concluded that medications work better for physicians who believe in them, than for those who are not enthused about them.

For the professional who wrote that deprecating word over the prayer report, prayer will not be an effective therapy. So for him or her, the castigation is valid, albeit unsocial.

If the reader would like to learn on the next few pages how to help their physician to help them, then the reader will be acquiring what might well be life extending skills.

On the other hand, if the reader has been mentally writing that 8-letter word on these pages up until now, then these next two pages can be a waste of time. Disbelief is negative mind-speak. It says, "Don't."

Positive belief enables your brain neurons to contact your body cells and encourage their normality. Positive mind-speak.

Here is how, step-by-step.

1. Sit in a comfortable chair and close your eyes.

2. Relax by taking a few deep breaths.

3. Deepen your relaxation by being aware of different parts of your body – scalp, forehead, eyes – from head to toes, and relaxing these parts.

4. Imagine yourself in some peaceful place you can remember, a tranquil scene that you enjoy.

5. Pretend you are able to go into your body. In fact, you are able to be at the trouble spot in your body. Be aware of it. "See it."

6. Make corrections in your imagination. (More on this next.)

7. "See" any medications you might be taking working well. Love your cells and organs.

8. Imagine the trouble spot totally corrected and no longer trouble. "See" everything normal, healthy as it should be.

9. Tell yourself that when you open your eyes at the count of three, you will be wide awake feeling great.

10. Count to three, open your eyes, re-affirm your feeling great.

HOW TO ENCOURAGE YOUR IMMUNE SYSTEM TO ROUT OUT THE "INVADERS"

The above ten steps comprise both the Simonton Method and the Silva Method. Dr. Simonton took the Silva Method training albeit by another name, while he was oncologist at Travis Air Force Base.

He decided to adopt it for his cancer patients. Because of the practice by military bases of sharing their experiences through periodic reports, Simonton's dramatic rate of success and decrease in cure time became of more than passing interest.

The first step does not appear as number one above. It was covered just before the steps were spelled out. It entails expectation and belief.

To rev up belief in getting well, usually at a low ebb in cancer patients, Simonton had the patient view a half hour or hour of slides of cancer cures. Now you see it, now you don't. The family was also asked to view these slides as their belief system was part of the consciousness "climate."

Let's examine step 6, making corrections in your imagination.

Although the Silva Method is being used daily around the world for helping the body to normalize the whole spectrum of physical and mental abnormality, it is the Simonton experience with cancer that provides the most documented approaches.

The elimination of cancer from the body is the job of the immune system. The white blood corpuscles or cells that act as the internal security guards.

The cancer patient is encouraged to imagine he or she is inside the body and exhorting the guards to do battle with the invaders. However the patient "sees" this does not matter.

One patient saw the white blood cells as a snowstorm sweeping away the dead and dying cells after a radiation treatment.

A young boy "saw" his white blood cells as cowboys on horses riding herd on the cancer cells.

An Air Force navigator saw his white blood cells as navy frogmen swimming after and capturing the cancer cells.--a picture they thought was rather disloyal of him.

Some patients shy away from a "give battle" approach and prefer a more permissive, loving mental message. Same positive result.

No matter how you "see" the normal good health returning is fine. You do not have to be anatomically precise, for it is the concept of restoring health that is the message given the cells.

They "hear" that message. They react.

Call that reaction the Backster Effect or the Simonton Effect or the Silva Effect or celebrate when it works for you by giving the Effect your name.

The medical practitioners call it psychoneuroimmunology.

By any name, it is a growing approach to getting well and staying well.

OTHER WAYS TO HELP YOUR BODY
BY USING YOUR MIND

It is a mistake to think that this communication between mind and body is only possible when you go through those ten steps. Mind-body communication is on-going day and night.

The mind runs the body. When the body runs in a less than normal way, it is usually because the mind interfered.

Interference with the mental climate for good health is usually in the form of stress. Stress is any negative load on our attitudes and emotions. Anxiety, fear, jealousy, insecurity, loneliness, grief and worry are just a few of the mental products of a modern world.

We can also interfere with negative statements and negative experiences.

Our speech is full of "commands" to our cells and our organs:

"She gives me a pain in the neck."

"He galls me."

"I can't stand him."

"She makes me sick."

Each statement is an order, especially effective if repeated. Coming up: one pain in the neck, one gallstone, one bad ankle, one combination plate.

How fortunate that subjective communication works to make us sick! Because, it can also be used to make us well.

You can siphon the fluid from your lovable lungs and "see" them perfect. That is a "command."

You can crush the kidney stone with your fingers and "see" it dissolving in the urine.

You can give your white blood cells a loving pep talk and chase away the cold virus.

You can apply an imaginary "tumor shrinker salve" and "see" the tumor disappearing.

All of these are the mind lovingly doing what it does naturally – make you well.

However you conceive it, you relieve it.

SCIENCE IS FORCED OUT OF ITS OWN ACCEPTED BOUNDARIES--BY LOVE

Oneness with one's own cells? Sharing consciousness with your family and neighbors? Using love and togetherness to communicate subjectively, higher self to higher self? Enter a tune-in and a turn-on: love.

Is love scientific?

Hardly. Certainly not today. But it may well be tomorrow.

If love is necessary to communicate in the non-physical world, then religions, which act as a conduit between this world and that, should reflect love in their teaching. One does not have to go very far to find this to be so.

In Islam: "Love is this, that thou shouldst account thyself very little and God very great."

In Buddhism: "Let a man cultivate towards the whole world a heart of love."

In Judaism: "Thou shalt love thy neighbor as thyself."

In Christianity: "He that loveth not, knoweth not God, for God is love."

In Shinto: "Love is the representative of the Lord."

In Hinduism: "One can best worship the Lord through love."

There is one former agnostic; pertinent to this book, whose research into primary perception brought about a change in his philosophical beliefs.

"I used to be pretty much a disbeliever," states Cleve Backster in an interview a few years into his work with plants. "I was an agnostic who didn't take the trouble to be an atheist. But now if you asked me, I'd have to reflect newly acquired insight regarding what higher levels of spirituality really entail."

He is not alone. Many scientists are beginning to sense a larger intelligence – perhaps a field of intelligence that fills all space. Says Dr. Edgar Mitchell, seventh astronaut on the moon, "We have to begin to hypothesize that there is a spiritual basis to the physical world."

Amen.

Footnotes:

[1] September 6, page 168

[2] May 16, page 418

[3] With C.I. Howland

Chapter VI

Backlash From The Scientific Community

"We have no evidence that this is valid."

These appear to be strong words. They tend to refute all positive evidence. They are the most common words used by professionals in any discipline where the status quo is challenged.

In fact, they are not strong words. They are weak words. What they are really saying is, "We know nothing about this. We have never looked into it. We have no experience with it." But the kiss off statement above better hides your ignorance.

How many professional researchers could possibly have monitored human cells at a distance from the donor's body and come up with evidence that the Backster Effect is valid? Not many. How many have experienced Remote Viewing or taken the Silva Method training and found themselves to be psychic? Not many.

All the rest can truthfully say that they have no evidence that any of these are valid and each single handedly stall off human progress.

Every new physical theory has its attackers. Every new medical approach has its opponents. Every philosophical gem has its detractors. It is as if consciousness is a giant gyroscope, set in its current plane and able to resist forces intent on altering that plane.

Of course it is not a gyroscope in action but one of the important characteristics of a gyroscope – stability.

For the world to benefit by the consciousness raising forces that now seem evident, it must not permit the forces of stability to demand one step backwards for each step forward.

Occasionally, Mr. and Mrs. John Q. Public must take matters into their own hands to insure their rights to new knowledge and new abilities. They have demonstrated their ability to do this quite admirably where threats to the environment have endangered their survival. They have fought for protection against radiation, toxic waste, and pollution to air and water. They have campaigned for the clean-up of beaches and harbors. They have legislated their right to air free of cigarette smoke.

Now they must recognize consciousness pollution. As consciousness becomes enlightened, it becomes fair target for perpetrators of impurity.

The advanced Tucker car was doomed from the start. Nylon stockings, shear and strong to begin with, cut down on the hosiery business and so their strength was reduced. Nichola Tesla's ideas revolutionized electric power generation, but it threatened vested interests, so it went down the drain. The status quo in each case won. We lost.

In order to better recognize the scientific personality and so to better evaluate its being for or against the enlightenment of consciousness, it is valuable to study scientific opposition in action.

THE SOLUTION THAT WAS SO DILUTED
IT APPEARED TO DILUTE THE TRUTH

Quoting Edgar Mitchell again, "There are no unnatural or supernatural phenomena, only very large gaps in our knowledge of what is natural...We should strive to fill those gaps of ignorance."

The problem is that when someone succeeds in filling a gap, it tends to substantiate the unnatural or supernatural. The human hackles go up and gorges rise.

Take the case of the impossible dilute solution.

In 1987, a French scientist, D. Jacques Benveniste, produced a solution so dilute that less than a molecule of the drug was present, yet it produced the same result as a stronger solution. Less than a molecule means none of the drug could be in solution. How could no drug present produce the same effect as some drug present?

His paper sat with the British journal *Nature* more than a year before they dared to publish it, but even then with the editorial comment that the conclusions were "unbelievable" and had "no physical basis."

The fact that Benveniste had 13 international researchers collaborating with him on the paper convinced the editors that fraud could not be a factor.

But, the fact that some were involved in the homeopathic approach to healing where minute doses of a substance are used in therapy gave them pause. This approach is not scientifically accepted and these dilute solution results could, in the eyes of the editors, give aid and comfort to the "enemy."

Then again, the fact that Benveniste is a respected researcher at INSERM, the equivalent in France to the U.S. National Institutes of Health, and was offered the post of minister of health by French President Mitterand, the editors went ahead and published the paper.

The backlash from the scientific community was immediate and energetic.

To the scientific mind, molded by the paradigms of Newtonian physics, the idea of a solution being so diluted as to preclude the presence of even one molecule of the additive was abnoxious. It was abnoxious because it was illogical and incredible. More than that it was impossible.

To back their "impossible" contestion, a self-appointed investigative team received permission to view the performance of the controversial experiment. They included *Nature* editor John Maddox, fraud investigator Walter Stewart, and professional magician James Randi.

The latter has devoted much of his time in recent years to tracking down all claims of the supernormal and pointing them up as deception – far from an open scientific view.

What followed was a four-page article in *Nature* declaring their findings. The original report appeared in the June 30, 1988 issue; the follow-up report appeared in the July 28, 1988 issue. Such speed in the publishing business requires pre-meditated, pre-planned and probably pre-conceived results.

According to Benveniste, the investigation was more of a witch-hunt than a sober search for scientific truth. He was quoted in the newspaper *Le Monde* as saying that because none of the three had a background in immunology, there were numerous mistakes and misunderstandings in the investigation. "This was nothing but a real scientific comedy, a parody of an investigation carried out by a magician and a scientific prosecutor working in the purest style of...McCarthyist or Soviet ideology."

There followed more backlash and backlash to the backlash.

At least one medical journal criticized *Nature* for undertaking verification through their own investigation – a possible conflict of interest. An independent scientific group should have been used.

The Randi report branded Benveniste's work as auto-suggestion, statistically poorly controlled, with no effort to exclude systematic error or observer bias.

Another "We have no evidence that this is valid."

And another opportunity lost to "fill those gaps of ignorance."

THE "IMPOSSIBLE" IS NOW
GENERATING A CHANGE OF MIND

Let us take a closer look at this experiment.

The purpose was to test whether individuals are allergic to certain material such as dust or pollen. White blood cells from the individual to be tested are combined in a test tube with the suspect material.

If the test is positive, the cells will react with the substance. A dye is used to see if this reaction has occurred. If it has, the cells cannot be stained by the dye. So by counting the cells that have changed color, the results are obtained.

The solution was diluted to see if the reaction still took place. It did. The dilution was continued even more to see at what point no allergic reaction would result. After 120 tenfold dilutions, the reactions still took place. It was a dilution that meant not even one molecule of the substance – the basic material unit – was present!

Theoretically, the substance was still creating its effect without being there.

This is not the first time science has been faced with the "impossible." Ask Copernicus, Planck, and Einstein.

The true scientist, paraphrasing Mitchell, is one who sees the impossible not necessarily as an error in the procedures, but rather as a possible missing link in our knowledge.

Enter the true scientists into the case of the impossible dilute solution. They came to the rescue of the "impossible..."

Benveniste, who finds it difficult himself to believe in his own results, is heartened by the fact that researchers in five other laboratories, mostly outside of France, have verified his findings on 70 separate occasions.

What seems to be the most accepted explanation by a consensus of the researchers involves one small step in the experiment: The solution is vigorously shaken for at least ten seconds at each progressive dilution.

Without this ten seconds of vigorous shaking, the "impossible" does not take place, which of course points the finger at this shaking as a clue.

Simply stated by the scientists, the agitation of the solution imparts the substance's potential effect to the water.

It is as if the water acquires "knowledge" of the substance. Water molecules might have a sort of "template" that recorded in its own electro-magnetic field the chemical characteristics of the substance.

As a post-script to this scientific tempest in a test tube, other scientists have come forward in other projects confirming the same phenomena:

A University of Pittsburgh project has observed that one dosage of a drug continues to affect the body long after any residue could possible remain.

Also, six other substances were tested and found to produce their effects when so diluted that none could still be present.

Homeopathic physicians have long been treating diseases with small quantities of natural chemicals that cause much the same symptoms of the disease. In some cases the dosage is so small that it contains only a few molecules, not enough to have a measurable effect according to accepted practice. But it still works.

Homeopathic pharmacists also shake a mixture violently for at least ten seconds. They call this succusion. Benveniste now sees this agitation as enabling the chemical to leave its imprint on the water – a sub-molecular re-organization of the water. It is this imprint on the water which causes the same reaction to take place as if the chemical was still there.

This is a change of mind. It takes into account the energy

realm, which is the creative realm for matter. It is literally a quantum leap.

It will effect medical care. It will benefit people. The cost? A few temporarily deflated egos. Like Randi's.

OPPOSITION TO THE "IMPOSSIBLE" BACKSTER EFFECT

The Backster Effect has been stalled on a siding.

When it was first publicized, it brought in a record number of inquiries from scientists all over the world. Few looked at it, though, as the promise of millions in foundation money. But, talking to plants? It was worth a million dollars of satisfying scientific curiosity.

When these interested scientists failed to produce the Backster Effect, they lost interest. The reason they failed was that, instead of using spontaneity in triggering a plant response, the scientists "told" the plants ahead of time that they would use a protocol.

Protocol, in plant language, means this is not for real.

Attacks on Backster up until now have been sporadic and few. He has been immersed in his mouth cell research with his associate Stephen White. He is not interested in publicity but rather in the development of a volume of decisive data that the scientific community cannot sweep under the bed. He is a serious, honest researcher and what he sees happening on his split screen television is too world-shaking to risk putting a chip on his professional shoulder.

This book, a primetime network television appearance, and a few currently scheduled major talks promise to change that.

Backster's message will be fascinating tidings for many, perturbing tidings for others.

Was that a knock on the door? Who's there? Randi? Randi who?

In the early 1980's, American geophysicists drilled a one mile deep hole in the Greenland ice at a U.S. Air Force radar station some 60 miles south of the Arctic Circle. Their purpose was to obtain ice containing air specimens from ages ago. Then, in the summer of 1988, other researchers lowered a 300-pound weight down the 4-inch diameter hole to see the effect of gravity at various distances. To their amazement, the measurements were several percentage points stronger than they were supposed to be.

The reaction of the scientists as reported in the press was, "We tried like hell to make it go away, but it just wouldn't."

Whether or not scientists are going to "try like hell" to make the Backster Effect go away, is problematical.

Actually, those Arctic findings have led to the discovery of a force in addition to gravity which makes Newton's 300-year-old law not entirely right. It is like a larger intelligence was raising humankind's consciousness by leading us gently by the hand to more sources of insight into that intelligence's own existence.

The Backster Effect could be one of those sources of insight. It demands a change of mind. The change can be succinctly put as: space is not nothingness – space is somethingness.

There has been quite a lift in consciousness in the past two decades since Backster's work "hit the fan." The outcry about plants was loud. The outcry about cells will be a lot less vociferous. The change of mind that it demands is already underway.

VOICES THAT STILL CRY OUT AGAINST CHANGE

In 1986 an article appeared in a national newspaper "down under" called the *Weekend Australian.*. In it, writer Phillip Adams stated quite definitively that the work of Cleve Backster had been discredited. There was found to be a "wiring fault" in his equipment.

The accusation found its way to Backster via an Australian member of the Theosophical Society who wrote to the director of the Krotona Institute, a theosophical school where Backster was scheduled to lecture. This member noted that Backster's would-be discreditor was a prominent man, part of a group that were actively challenging all ESP claims.

Backster replied to the theosophist's informative letter, saying,

"I find it somewhat amusing that it would be seriously thought that someone with my technical background would have over-looked, during an intensified twenty year period of research, a "wiring fault" in my equipment. The individuals you mention are either seriously uninformed or are trying to perpetrate the present limited scope of scientific knowledge by maintaining closed minds.

"I would like to suggest a non-confrontational approach to you. I am willing to supply you with reference material to give you more background relating to my research. If these people are operating with opened minds let them sponsor a visit by me to Australia.   If they are willing to cover all conventional travel expenses I am willing to contribute my time. If they decline they obviously are not interested in being informed. This would make it easier for you to refute their rather negative approach to non-materialist phenomena."

Backster's offer was not accepted by his challengers.

Right from the start of his research, Backster sought to avoid such confrontations by carefully side-stepping the term Extra-sensory perception (ESP). He felt it was not "extra," that it was basic to organisms. So he used the term "primary perception," the word "primary" actually refuting the word "extra."   But the antagonists to ESP still feel threatened.

Another researcher, who intuitively felt that this ability in humans was not extra when he developed a simple training to activate it, is Jose Silva. In his course vocabulary, it is called Effective Sensory Projection – the ability of humans to project their intelligence anywhere and perceive information that they have no way of knowing through the usual sensory channels.

So, to look at the Backster Effect in plants or human cells through Jose Silva's eyes, these also have the ability to project their intelligence at a distance.

The similarity of the concepts of primary perception and effective sensory projection is compelling. They deserve a single term to describe both. However, because primary perception is derived from the cell's point-of-reference and effective sensory projection from the human mind point-of-reference an insur-mountable dichotomy prevents a unified term.

What is the answer? As researchers zero in on this phenome-non from different points-of-reference even though they agree are they to be separated by semantics?

Sadly, yes. Agreement can appear as disagreement. Backster may be attacked by other researchers discovering the same phenomenon but, because theirs is a different point-of-reference, using different terminology and then fighting for their share in the professional battle of territorial imperative and recognition. This is far from the case with Silva and Backster; they understand each other's language and are mutual supporters.

But, of course, the loudest voices will be those of the entrenched opponents to anything remotely connected to the paranormal.

DOES A LARGER INTELLIGENCE
HAVE A SAY IN THE MATTER?

If a change of mind is underway – if collective human intelligence is beginning to recognize its common all pervasive source – not only will the confrontations be fewer but certainly less vitriolic.

Evidence of this has already been quite adequately presented in "The Greening of America" and "The Aquarian Conspiracy." Your author has added his own "licks" in previous chapters and will continue to do so in the chapters ahead.

The raising of human consciousness appears to be accelerating. Its effects are not only on the physical side – such as moving from speeds of 10 miles an hour to 10,000 miles per hour in less than a century. But it is also on the non-physical, as exploration into outer space and inner-space reaches beyond classical physical frontiers into the realm of fields, systems, forces and energy. See Chapter VIII.

Health frontiers are expanding into new horizons of holistic therapies that boggle the minds of physicians practicing in the conventional vein. This is covered in more detail in the next chapter VII.

Something else is happening that gives even the author pause and he is a man who has undergone several changes of mind. This "something else" appears in a number of ways, all of which are outside of physical comprehension, and which appear to have a built-in message: You are not alone. Three examples:

1. Synchronicity. Things happen that have a connection. Maybe an inane connection, but still some connection. For instance, you talk about a mutual friend you have not seen in years. A few hours later you bump into him. Or you get a letter from someone in Bird-in-Hand, Pennsylvania, the day after you ate in a restaurant by the same name a thousand or more miles away. When you become aware of synchronicity, it seems to happen with unnerving frequency, and repeating, "You are not alone."

2. Channeling. More and more individuals are able to go into a meditative state and appear to have a heightening of intelligence. They attribute this wisdom to an entity in another realm for which they themselves are merely the channel. For instance, *A Course in Miracles*, 1500 pages containing a spiritual exercise for each day of the year came "through" the late Dr. Helen Schucman in the mid-1960's while serving on the staff of Columbia University's Presbyterian Hospital. She wrote without pondering. It was like an inner dictation. It was in iambic pentameter. Even if the phone rang in the middle of a sentence, when she returned she continued without missing a beat!

The basic message was that the physical world is an illusion. We must forgive and love in order to enjoy miracles from the creative realm which is the reality. Although a "card carrying" skeptic, nobody knew better than Dr. Schucman, after taking those 1500 pages of dictation, that she was not alone.

3.Uniting. Movements for togetherness are springing up. Like networking, and coalitions. It is crossing national boundaries with more people-to-people contacts. Society is concentrating less on differences and more on samenesses. Confrontation is less and less and cooperation more and more. Groups and factions and races are coming together almost in spite of themselves, as if an outside influence was nudging them.

If the author was asked to prove scientifically that we were not alone, how could he go about it?

Even the convincing results of Dr. Rupert Sheldrake in demonstrating the existence of a larger computer into which our mental computer is "plugged in," will not satisfy the die-hards.

"We have no evidence that this is valid."

The author is not frustrated at his inability to satisfy the Randis of the world. The author is not in charge of creation, just responsible for a minute piece of it. Metamorphosis is happening and cannot be stopped. The growth of consciousness, like any growth, is inexorable.

Occasionally there will be a man like Backster or Benveniste who will demonstrate beyond a shadow of a doubt that there is something out there that we cannot deny. When that happens the Randis eat crow. Their flamboyance recedes.

It's as if some larger intelligence says, "Enough."

Let us call it the "Oh, Yeah?" Law.

Synchronicity, channeling and uniting are not events that are suitable for the microscope, the telescope, or other scientific efforts to analyzc, dissect, or trace. They are phenomena associated with the energy of human consciousness.

When the author received his training at the Massachusetts Institute of Technology (M.I.T.), the existence of an energy called consciousness was not acknowledged. A half century later he received the first doctorate ever awarded in Psychotronics which is the study of the energy of consciousness.

We have thoroughly charted the world of the seen. Now comes the world of the unseen.

It's a whole new ball of wax.

GETTING THE "IMPOSSIBLE" ACROSS INTELLIGIBLY TO THE MEDIA

The popular press will play a key role in the metamorphosis of consciousness. As more and more people understand more and more about their potential abilities, the manifestation of these abilities will accclerate.

Prior to 1954, athletes believed that running the mile in four minutes or less was an impossibility. Nobody did it. Four minutes was similar to the sound barrier for runners. Then Roger Bannister broke that barrier. He ran the mile in less than four minutes. Immediately, the other athletes were able to match or better his record.

That barrier was not a sound barrier. It was a consciousness barrier.

What Bannister did for runners, the press can do for the public. But will they do it? Will they assist in removing limiting beliefs or will they insist on perpetuating thcm?

The answer lies in part with the scientists like Backster who are in the frontier where the possible meets thc impossible. IIow well are these researchers able to communicate their findings to thc non-scientist reporter or writer?

Scientists make mistakes. So do reporters. Just as reporters are being exposed to the researcher's findings for the first time, so are the researchers quite likely being exposed to the press for the first time.

The loser is the public. The story, barely grasped by the reporter, loses more in the writing, and becomes of little value to the reader.

Researchers need to understand the reporter's needs. The scientific stance is in direct opposition to the media stance.

Science findings are tiny steps forward, presented in ambiguous and qualified ways which keep the scientist's head off the chopping block.

But the reporter is paid to discover dramatic new break-throughs that will revolutionize the world.

Who wins? The reporter. He is in charge of the words. Those words may have had to be slanted, bent or magnified to produce an interesting story. So the story itself becomes slanted, bent, or exaggerated and the public's lesson for the day is less than valid.

The public's classroom is the media. Education of the public is essential to scientists. The public funds their projects. They demand a share of the drama and excitement as well as the new knowledge and advantages that may be available to them as a result.

There needs to be an effort on the part of both sides – the researchers and the reporters – to help each other. The re-searcher could prepare his material in advance in non-technical words, perhaps with the use of public relations word-smiths. The reporter could do his homework and arrive with some foundation on which to build his story.

Researchers can help raise the level of science reporting by understanding the problems of reporters.

A CASE HISTORY OF BIASED REPORTING

The author has had experience in newspaper reporting, editing, and public relations. Yet, he found himself involved in a press bruha-ha quite recently.

He had given a public lecture on the advantages of activating the right hemisphere of the brain. He did not know that it was attended by a local columnist whose approaches are frequently caustic and critical. His article appeared in a Sunday edition entitled, "Anyone with half a brain shouldn't read this."

The columnist went on to lampoon the audience (fifty brain wasters); the subject (14 atoms in use at any one moment); and the author ("I did not have the brains to stick around.")

The author did not even go across town to confront this uninformed reporter. He decided to fight fire with fire and had a letter to the editor published in the same paper.

He told the columnist that using more of our mind, especially the creative right hemisphere, is not a matter to be made light of.

In his reporting of the Hawaii scene has he found empty prisons and empty hospitals?

"How far has his left brain taken him in life?..I used to be a journalist; then I activated my right hemisphere...I am now the author of 73 published books with millions of copies in print in six languages."

When Jose Silva was faced with having a reporter call him a fraud, he decided to go to Boston to confront his editor. As a result, another reporter actually took the training and wrote such a laudatory article that it became one of Silva's best pieces of promotional literature.

Fire with fire.

There is a lightning ready to strike. It is a personal lightning that contains flashes of insight and flames of inspiration.

How to trigger that lightning is one of our missing links. For some it happens quite accidentally. For others it comes when the electric potential has been enhanced by an improved self-image and heightened expectation and belief.

For Cleve Backster it was accidental. His curiosity as to how long the process of osmosis took from roots to leaves for a two-foot plant, led to his discovery of primary perception--one of the few clues acquired by science that leads to the world of the unseen.

As Helen Schucman was a non-believer in her own channeling, Backster was a non-believer in what he was apparently discovering.

The universe might have been saying to each, "Oh, yeah?"

Its own brand of backlash.

THE PROFESSIONAL IVORY TOWER–
A TOWER OF BABEL?

The Scottish poet Robert Burns wished that some power might "the giftie gie us to see ourles as others see us."

Scientists often adopt an ivory tower attitude. They throw up a separation between themselves and society that they may appear to be breed apart.

They are not the only professionals that do this. Many attorneys are barricaded behind lines of secretarial defense. Physicians often feel aloof and apart from their patients. As a result, communication between them, already hindered by a different vocabulary, can deteriorate further.

A hospital receptionist answered a switch board call.

"I would like to know the condition of Mrs. Smith in room 423."

The receptionist checked and told her, then asked, "May I know who is calling?"

"I am Mrs. Smith in 423. My doctor never tells me anything."

Many researchers must work in secrecy. That can be the name of the game. There is no issue there. But, synthetic ivory towers for the sake of creating an image inhibit professional growth and contribute nothing to the progress of science.

Less controversy, less conflict, less backlash would have a chance to build up if there were fewer ivory towers. Communications would flow. Inspiration would be more frequently triggered. Goals could be more rapidly reached.

Cleve Backster is disarming in his willingness to share the details of his work. He often puts aside important preparations when an impromptu visitor appears to see primary perception in action. This has often led to support from unexpected directions.

This open attitude resulted in a chapter devoted to him in *The Secret Life of Plants* and later another chapter devoted to him in *Star Signs* by Linda Goodman.

The latter mentioned his work with Stephen White on human oral leukocytes and triggered a flurry of letters expressing interest in and moral support for the work. As a result, a number of schools became aware of his work as did editors of other publications.

It has been pointed out for decades that nature abhors a vacuum. Today nature has acquired another pet peeve: separation.

Separation contributes to the stifling of ideas. Fraternization contributes to the interchange of ideas. Inhabitants of this world's ivory towers could very well be protecting existing dogmas or brewing new ones that they hope will bear their name.

Open researchers like Backster are chipping away at the walls of separation. The result is bound to be a more common language and therefore better communications.

The public will become more science oriented.

They may even begin to hear the tiny voice called primary perception.

FEAR AS A MOTIVATOR OF CONFLICT

If the energy involved in one scientist's attack on another

could be channeled instead to his own creativity, the world would benefit.   Not that wholesome controversy cannot in itself be creative, it just usually is not. It is seldom even wholesome.

Many attacks derive from a fear that one's own turf is being violated. If the other fellow is right, there may be some doubt thrown on your own validity. This triggers a fear of loss of reputation, and that could be followed by a loss of funds.

This is often extended beyond the scope of the researcher's findings into the area of the researcher's philosophy. Anything that tends to prove that a philosophy could be found wanting, creates a fear. It is a fear that borders on insecurity.

Fear of loss of reputation, fear of loss of grant money, fear of insecurity--these are just a few of the many fears that incite a professional researcher to question the findings of another.

Backster's approach is fearless, and might even be considered naive by battle-scarred researchers. Certainly it is disarming.

Here he is September, 1987, in Wichita, Kansas, speaking to the 10th International Conference on Human Functioning:

"I see parallels with (a previous speaker) in some of the work I have been doing in that the clues that have been uncovered seem to point in a direction that is extremely obvious until you are confronted with the body of scientific knowledge that is being perpetuated by present scientists. They can't beat you down, so they ignore you. That's their defense methodology.

"It could be frustrating. But I know that if we just keep working away, eventually the allied aspects of that scientific body will catch up to where we are and it will all make more sense. We will at least pave the way with a cutting edge."

The further into the unseen that researchers delve, the harder it becomes to bring back evidence into the physical world that is irrefutable. It can all be demolished by a single stentorian voice calling out from the scientific throng, "Bullshit!"

If even safe researchers want to play it safer out of fear of professional "decapitation," how do not-so-safe researchers handle their fears? Very difficultly. You have to be some sort of a hero, perhaps fearless.

THE HOPE OF THE PEOPLE:
PHILOSOPHERS OF SCIENCE

Backster has been keeping meticulous records and documentation of his work for many years. He is so conscientious in this regard that he has not usually been the target of those hard-core keepers of the faith who respect his meticulousness.

They also respect his unrivaled reputation as the topmost authority on the polygraph. It is hard to call a researcher with such an enviable reputation in one field, crazy in another field.

In the 1960's and the 1970's he had learned to cope with sincere people who wanted to replicate his work but did not have the right scientific training or did not fully grasp the importance of automation to eliminate the "x" factor of their own consciousness.

He has also learned to cope with authorities like Arthur Galston who was less open-minded than he was opposed to the basic premise on which primary perception is based. He is able to cope, too, with such publicity as a newspaper story that claimed "the Backster Effect is caused by the soles of your shoes creating static on the floor." The source of that discovery which went out over the wire services was another scientist whose daughter's school science fair project claimed to show this.

Another authority was J.B. Rhine, so-called father of parapsychology. Rhine invited Backster to join his research activities some years after he left Duke University. After Backster declined this offer, he noticed Rhine's enthusiasm became somewhat elusive.

Backster has learned to cope with such events as were involved the 1975 AAAS meeting, after which his offering of tape supplemental material appeared not to have been circulated to members. At the conference, an attempt was made to withold 200 packets of information for the press.

That meeting was a planned "shoot-out." Backster was the intended victim. The kill-off did not take place, thanks largely to Backster's having prepared a back-up 200 packets which made it to the press contingent via his own hands.

Take the National Research Council visit described at the start of Chapter I. Lt. Colonel John Alexander thought he was putting together an impartial committee. What he did not know was that what the Condon Committee was to UFOs, this committee was dedicated to be for plant biocommunications, particularly primary perception. It appears they had made up their minds in advance.

Their conclusion: "The Committee finds no scientific justification from research conducted over a period of 130 years for the existence of parapsychological phenomena."

Lt. Col. Alexander was horrified at their behavior. He was a serious researcher himself for many years and had successfully replicated Backster's white cell work. Soon after he resigned the Army in disgust.

Backster saw the committee's decision coming. An experienced interrogator, he recognized the unmistakable signs of intellectual constipation as they watched the split television screen. Some $500,000 of taxpayer's money had been spent to kill off what they did not believe in.

The public is the loser by more than money. Each backlash by scientist-bigots might eventually cost lives. Primary perception is one of the greatest promises to humanity for life extension. There is a conspiracy by vested scientific interests to bar it from our lives.

Backster is the finger in the dike.

"You are entirely too kind to scientists," said one seasoned scientist. "You are right to protect science, but scientists that misbehave do not merit your protection."

He voices the statesmanlike attitude of a breed of scientists, we do not hear very much about. They may be in universities or other institutions. They are the philosophers of science. They have no axe to grind except the scientific approach. They protect no branches or disciplines. They have access to university presses and the media, so they do have a voice.

Backster's experience to date adds up to a firm resolve to deal largely with these scientists. He will cooperate fully with them, while ignoring others. This does not mean he is painting all the others with the same brush, but part of the result of the backlash is he is cut off from foundation funds and he will not dilute his resources to feed potential detractors.

Backster's defense strategy is based on his dedication to truth and humanity. He will not be affected by the scientists' conspiracy of silence in the hopes he will go away. He will stay. He will continue his polygraph instruction and consultation work and his research into primary perception. He will publish first and talk to the media later. He has a vast army of popular media standing behind him and ready to support him. But as long as positive peer review is necessary for grant proposals, he will continue to function as best he can with self-funding, hoping for additional private support.

It is a solid defense strategy, based on his own primary perception.

A BUILT-IN ULTIMATE CONTROVERSY SUCCESS FACTOR FOR THE BACKSTERS OF THE SCIENTIFIC WORLD

In the earlier description of one aspect of right brain functioning – subjective communication – it was emphasized that a kinship, rapport or love needed to be felt for the message to get through. In other words, the right hemisphere functions best in a consciousness of unity rather than separation.

Fear separates. So any attempts to scientifically attack somebody else's findings for negative motives are unicameral thinking, that is, left-brained thinking, as opposed to bicameral thinking, that is, left *and* right-brained thinking.

Bicameral thinking is centered thinking. Unicameral thinking is not centered. It is off-centered. It is eccentric.

But even more critical is the fact that when you separate yourself from your fellow humans through attack, scientific or otherwise, you relegate yourself to the limits of the left hemisphere. Outside of those limits are the creative faculties. The right hemisphere connects us to those. So the eccentric thinker, with a consciousness of dichotomy, polarity, and duality, is sacrificing inspiration, intuition and insight.

What happens as an end result is the hostile critic may come out victorious with his or her resounding "Bull!", but the more friendly target of the onslaught comes out smelling like roses.

The author was interviewed recently in Hong Kong by a prestigious radio personality regarding right brain functioning. To his chagrin he was up against a totally disbelieving interviewer who made light of the right-brain, left-brain concept and blatantly called him a fraud.

The author replied with compassion and understanding. He appreciated the interviewer's regard for left-brain thinking in this left-brained world. He accepted the barbs as a necessary defense, while at the same time encouraging the interviewer to check out the latest scientific findings.

On the surface, it appeared to be a public relations fiasco for the author. But it turned out to be just the opposite. Listeners were drawn to him. Positive callers greatly outnumbered negative callers. The interview made him many new friends and supporters.

Is the lesson to welcome attacks? Of course not, but the lesson is certainly to maintain a fearless feeling of brotherhood no matter what. This keeps you "plugged in" to the source of creativity and inspiration. Backster knows this intuitively.

He emerges as a statesman.

WHERE YOUR CELLS STAND
IN THE CONTROVERSY

Wait a minute, you insist. If togetherness and fearlessness are characteristics of the creative realm, how come Backster uses fear-like emotions with his donors? And are not the recipient cells separated from these donors? Two miles or just across the room is not "together."

You have just put your finger on a clue as to the nature of primary perception.

Our consciousness is conditioned by the physical world to see it as the reality. A wall is green and a wall is hard. Actually the wall is anything but green. We see it as green because it repels light of that frequency reflecting back to us so it only appears green. Neither is it hard, its atoms having as much space between nucleus and orbiting electrons relatively as the sun and orbiting planets.

It is the world behind the world that is real. Ask your cells. We have to shift gears to get there. They are already there, being of both worlds.

They are hurt when a hammer hits them. They are hurt when negative energy hits them.

Primary perception takes place in the energy realm. It is the causal or creative realm. Using electrical energy as a bridge between that realm and the physical realm, Backster has stumbled on a way to make goings-on in the creative realm detectable in the physical realm.

This nauseates classical scientists. They would rather not attempt to "digest" it.

But it gives the rest of us food for thought.

All we have to do is learn how to shift gears from left to right brain and we are able to cross the bridge from the physical to the creative realm.

We are then in touch with our cells.

Our cells love it.

Just the way mung beans sprout faster if we send them mental love and support, as compared to an ignored control batch, so our lung cells, liver cells, mouth cells, blood cells respond to love and support.

As the next chapter describes in detail, we are in touch with our body's cells. This primary perception is two-fold. We provide a continuous climate for their growth, be it a pure or polluted climate. We can also provide a focused communication for correction of abnormalities and restoration of health.

Chapter VII
Holistic Health Implications

About a decade ago, scientists made a dramatic discovery about simple alga that grows in ponds. They found it could "see."

Although it does not, of course, have eyes, the one-celled plant of the species Chlamydomonas has a light sensitive "eyespot." This enables it to sense the amount of light in the water and to steer itself toward the light source or away from it to find the best level of light for photosynthesis.

The team of scientists from Columbia University and the City University of New York, found that the "eyespot" uses the same light-sensitive chemical that is in your eyes and mine, a visual pigment called rhotopsin.

But then the team ran into a problem. The algae have two hair-like flagella that act as human arms, when doing the breast stroke. These flagella steer the algae toward the light if too little light, away from the light, if too much. The scientists could detect the signal, a burst of atoms that were electrically charged, but they could not detect any chain of reactions, chemical or otherwise, that controlled the flagella.

So, they could only assume that such a chain of reactions existed and that somehow the flagella were getting the message.

The Backster Effect is certainly a simple explanation. It has been demonstrated on every cell-type tested, be it a one-celled self-sufficient organism or a complicated, advanced human cell. But it is currently a professionally unpopular one.

The use of the Backster Effect in explaining physiological cause-effect relationships promises to relieve scientists of unexplained quandaries and bail them out of prisons of frustrating dead-end research.

The Backster Effect says that cells have a primary perception. Let us look at what happens when scientists take it from there.

THE SEARCH FOR THE CHAIN OF COMMAND

Today there is mounting scientific evidence pointing to our state of mind being a powerful influence over whether we fall prey to disease or not. The big news is:

The first clues have been uncovered as to how the mind can alter the workings of the body to either harm us or heal us.

The key to the above statement being newsworthy is the word "how." For a century or more, the big word was "if." Since the evidence of a brain/body connection has mounted, the "if" has given way to "how."

The first clues as to "how" are not all that exciting. And they may never be. Yes, the brain and the immune system have a two-way communication going. That communication has been demonstrated again and again, but the scientific details of just how that communication works remains theory and guesswork.

For instance, it is now thought possible that the hypothalamus and neocortex in the brain may house the transmission mechanism for messages to the immune system. But what is the immune system/nervous system connection? The answer to that question continues to elude the investigators.

The difficulty, they explain, is largely due to the immune system not having a clearly defined boundary. It does not appear to have a central headquarters. It is an army of cells on constant patrol against alien micro-organisms, but an army apparently without a commander or a chain of command. Rather, it is run by an intelligent strategy that reaches to each white blood cell soldier in that army wherever in the body it happens to be.

If a white cell from the mouth – even when removed yards away from its home base – can react to the brain's stress or excitement, is it not plausible to suggest that the Backster Effect might be the elusive immune system/nervous system connection?

IS THIS SEARCH REALLY NECESSARY?

A woman with a peaches-and-cream complexion acquires the only blemish to ever mar her face on her wedding day. You can bet that it is due to some emotion.

A young dental hygienist, afraid to leave home and live on her own, develops warts under her fingernails. Once she realizes the connection, they are easily eliminated through hypnosis.

A victim of a severe burn is asked by the physician to feel as though the burn is beginning to appear cool and comfortable. Instead of the usual skin grafting and extended recovery time, the patient recovers rapidly with no complications, no infection, no scar.

These three examples of the skin demonstrating the brain/body connection are offered by a national magazine as evidence that the skin, being closely linked to the nervous system, responds most readily to emotions.

But, in that same article, Harvard University psychiatrist Steven Locke is quoted as saying, "For the first time in the history of medicine, there dangles before us the tantalizing possibility of explaining the way the brain and mind make us sick or keep us healthy."

Aspirin, the most commonly used drug in the world, helps reduce pain, fever, inflammation and other unwanted conditions, yet the medical profession which recommends it does not fully understand how it works.

The drug purportedly most prescribed by doctors is not really a drug at all but is a sugar pill called the placebo. Because the patient believes he or she is receiving a legitimate remedy for the undiagnosed problem, the confident brain contacts the immune system and a cure takes place. Again, the medical profession does not fully understand how it works.

Why must they now demand an explanation for the way the mind affects our health? Can it be their hope is that such an explanation might afford a way to perpetuate the allopathic approach? Is primary perception and subjective communication a threat to the medical profession?

THE COST TO US OF THIS
UNNECESSARY SEARCH

You and I make ourselves sick. We fear, we worry, we hate, we feel insecure.The stress from these negative attitudes saps our immune system and we succumb to whatever virus or bacteria is around.

What do we do to make ourselves well? Do we seek ways to change our attitudes and emotions from negative to positive? No, we turn ourselves over to the doctor and say, "You do it."

Understandably, the doctors like it that way. They want to keep it that way and need to understand the chemical chain that comprises the brain/body connection.

But what if there is none? What if it is the Backster Effect at work? What if brain neurons communicate with white blood cells directly? The medical profession could be years looking for a chemical chain that does not exist.

Meanwhile, you and I will be deprived of sure-fire techniques to use our mind to activate our immune system, to correct other systemic abnormalities – to make ourselves well. The reluctance on the part of researchers to accept the already demonstrated, albeit unexplainable Backster Effect could be taking years off of our life expectancy.

OPERATION LEAP FROG: WE BEGIN
TO USE THE BRAIN/BODY CONNECTION

We do not fully understand electricity but we go ahead and use it. Fortunately, there is a growing number of health care specialists who see the importance of the brain/body connection and feel that the priority is to use it, rather than understand its physiology.

Operation Leap Frog has begun outside of standard medical circles. Holistic health circles are skipping over the identification of the chain of command in the brain/body connection and formulating mental techniques for correcting health problems,-- putting the connection to work now.

Some know about the Backster Effect and acknowledge it as a front runner in the race for an explanation. Some know about the Backster Effect and find it difficult to relate to at all. Most never heard of the Backster Effect.

It does not matter. Thanks to the Backster Effect, all three groups are making progress in using the brain to correct health problems. As a result, a major new approach to getting well and staying well is emerging.

In summarizing a recent showing of "INNOVATION" on the National Educational Television network, entitled "Mind Over Matter," announcer Jim Hartz said, "Whether science can ever completely explain the mysteries of mind over matter remains to be seen. Yet, already, doctors are beginning to harness together the powers of body and mind to heal the body from within."

Among the examples covered on the show were:

   * A man who once had skin cancer visualized his white cells standing vigilant against its return. He has been successful.

   * How the pressure of exams affect the immune system in medical students, and how positive visualization can alleviate this.

   * The use of visualization techniques for stress management halves the number of people needing drugs for high blood pressure.

Can we use our mind to "talk" to our body cells and is visualization the language of the mind? If so, then is visualization the way to start to use the brain/body connection?

"TALKING" THE LANGUAGE OF THE MIND

If the Backster Effect is an indication of the cells' mode of communication for both brain cells and body cells, then the answer to whether visualization is the key is both yes and no.

Yes, because mental pictures have been shown to affect cells under laboratory conditions. No, because other types of mental functions are also effective.

From the early plant observations, when the mere thought associated with intent of watering them brought a positive response, to the latest mouth cell experiments, when an unanswered phone brought an excited response, mental visualization has not been a required factor. Rather, it is an optional approach. A more general umbrella term covering all mental approaches that produces the Backster Effect might be said to be: mental conceptualizing.

The reason this point is emphasized now is that many people

who wish to benefit by activating the brain/body connection feel they cannot hold pictures in their mind.

The writer, being a lecturer in the Silva Method of Mind Control, has come across countless students who throw their mental hands up and say, "I can't see anything."

My reaction is often, "Do not picture what I am about to describe. Do not picture a white polar bear with a pink bikini." The resulting guffaw belies the professed inability.

I then ask the student to picture a "frenessie." Since this is a nonsense word, there is no mental concept. The student "sees" nothing.

Conceptualizing is the key.

VISUALIZATION VERSUS CONCEPTUALIZATION

Mental conceptualizing is therefore a less limiting way to describe what needs to be done mentally at the sending end. Conception sent is perception received.

Most of the Silva Method techniques require visualization. A student is asked to go inside the body, detect the health problem, and correct it.   Confronted with an "I can't", the instructor frequently says, "Imagine you are drawing the problem with crayon on a sketch pad." The resulting imagined drawing is often dramatically accurate. Brain neuron here to brain neuron there communication is not by usual sensory means.

Apparently distance is no barrier to the Backster Effect. A cell's primary perception may be more related to survival than to time or space.   The Silva Method demonstrates this when a student is asked to check out the health of a person in critical condition thousands of miles away.   It is "a piece of cake" compared to more minor illnesses.

At a recent session, the writer was called over to where a student had a problem with "seeing" somebody thousands of miles away. "I don't mentally see the person."

"Well, don't bother trying to see the person," I replied. "If you could readily conceive the person, what kind of a physical problem would the person have?"

Back came the reply, "Breast cancer." It was exactly right.

It was a guess. And it was right. Lucky? No, not luck--primary perception. It functions with or without visualization.

The Silva Method is no longer alone in uses of visualization, as it was for more than two decades. Many other disciplines, therapies and trainings are now using this same visualizing approach.

GROWING POPULARITY OF VISUALIZATION

Seminars on visualization are now being offered both on the professional and lay level. One that made the rounds of a number of cities in 1985 was titled, "Intensive Training in Guided Imagery" and presented by Marquette University and the Medical College of Wisconsin, with Donald M. Pachita, M.D. and Anees A. Sheikh, Ph.D., the seminar's faculty.

A look into the topics covered in this particular seminar is, in a way, a look into the future. Here are health professionals defying the resistance of their colleagues and boldly exploring the brain/body connection in a practical way. Some of the topics covered were:

* The nature of healing imagery;
* The power of imagery in the treatment of life-
    threatening illness;
* Techniques to enhance the imaging ability;
* The power of imagery in the treatment of
    chronic intractable pain;
* Imagery and spirituality

To scientists like Cleve Backster and Jose Silva, founder of Silva Mind Control, it is heartening to see health professionals honing up on how to have their patients and clients use imagery to improve communications between spouses; to manage stress; to control smoking and overeating; to enhance inner wisdom; and to help with such health problems as insomnia, asthma, headaches, skin disorder, phobias and depression.

To Silva, it is a mixed blessing. The costly decades of research that produced the Silva Method are paying off handsomely with hundreds of thousands of new graduates around the world each year; but the new spin-offs, adapted techniques and revised approaches recognized his work neither in principle nor financially.

To Backster it is also a mixed blessing. His decades of research have been equally solitary. He has been a lone voice crying that a primary perception exists between living cells. Now that the principle is in growing use, again there is little reference or cognizance of the involvement of the Backster Effect. And the particular use that is growing – mental imagery – is only the tip of the iceberg.

PSYCHONEUROIMMUNOLOGY:
BRAIN/BODY "BREAKTHROUGH"

Research continues to identify mental imagery as a significant ingredient in the therapeutic process; and as wider circles of health care professionals continue to harness the healing powers of mental imagery, it has been given its own nomenclature by the medical profession – more likely in the spirit of segregating it than in welcoming it. Certainly the number of professionals involved in psychoneuroimmunology are minute in comparison to other specialties.

As time passes and more skeptical colleagues see the successes, the "tribe" will certainly increase. Meanwhile it is getting its share of publicity in the popular media.

The theme of a recent article in *Readers' Digest*, April, 1987, entitled "Mind Over Disease" by Donald Robinson was, "...solid evidence that emotions, mental attitudes and coping all strongly affect the immune system." After reviewing the ebb and flow of the long dispute over the effects of a positive mental attitude, the article ended by quoting Dr. Isaac Djerassi, Director of Oncology at Mercy Catholic Medical Center in Philadelphia: "We now have convincing evidence that the right mental attitude can help your immune system function more effectively."

All of this is "kid stuff" to the researchers who are on the front lines. They are having burn victims visualize in such a way as to decrease infection and accelerate healing. Others are having heart attack victims visualize in such a way as to have the heart-feeding blood vessels clear any clogging. They are having cancer victims visualize the dead and dying cancer cells after radiation being captured and removed by the blood's white cells. They look at the dramatic health results and call psychoneuroimmunology a breakthrough.

But to pioneers such as Backster and Silva even these life-saving uses of psychoneuroimmunology are "kid stuff."

PERHAPS THE REAL BREAKTHROUGH
IS STILL TO COME

They see the big picture. Healing is a small part of it, albeit valuable. But when you see plant cells detect the difference between pre-planned thoughts and spontaneous thought, even at a distance; when you see bacterial cultures detect when other bacterial cultures are being fed; when you see the "in vitro" white cells react at a distance to the donor's excitement watching television violence, then body cells reacting to encouraging thoughts is just a small part of that big picture.

We mentioned earlier that at the Second World Psychotronic Conference in Monte Carlo in 1975, physicians reported when a drug in which the physician has little confidence is administered to his patient by him, the result is disappointing, as compared to that same drug being administered by a physician who has complete confidence in it. This points to the brain/body connection as going also from the brain of one person to the body of another.

This is a phenomenon that laughs at such intensive research now in progress as to how the immune system "talks" to the brain, with neuropeptides, macrophases and other polysyllabic entities at least tentatively credited with playing a role in the communications.

The "big picture" sees the communication as energetic rather than chemical. Backster, Silva and others of similar stature see the real breakthrough as understanding that special energy and how it works.

Is primary perception in the Backster Effect the tapping into a field of energy that is local? Or is it universal?

Is projecting one's intelligence with the Silva method really projecting? Or, is it also tapping into a universal field of energy?

SPACE: NOTHINGNESS OR INTELLIGENCE

When Dr. Edgar Mitchell returned to earth from his visit to the moon, he resolved to study consciousness. He had received his doctoral degree at the Massachusetts Institute of Technology. The author also having M.I.T. as his alma mater, can vouch for the fact that not only was consciousness not studied there in those years, but hardly recognized to exist. Of course, that is all now changed.

Mitchell founded the Institute for Noetic Sciences in 1973 to sponsor and co-sponsor research projects involving powers of the mind. These projects included at the outset, intensive looks at so-called mental telepathy – with or without Faraday cage (no barrier) – with or without a de-gaussing network (does not alter the signal); psycho-kinesis – moving objects with consciousness (magnetic instruments easiest); levitation and depression of weight with consciousness (recorded with electronic scale); psychic healing (hundreds of cases); dematerialization (caught on camera).

Describing the data collected by these projects, Mitchell says that to explain these phenomena one would have to go to a cosmology much closer to religion than to classical science. One would have to start hypothesizing that there is an ultimate consciousness field that permeates space and guides the universe. It would have to have intelligence and such properties as "intention, agreement, awareness;" he sees such a field as being affected by human consciousness. Just the way plasma can change a magnetic field by trapping magnetic lines of force, he says so might matter be affected by thought.

Can you see ears perking up, like those belonging to Backster, Silva et al?

The Institute for Noetic Sciences is headed at the present writing by Willis Harmon, Ph.D., a member of the California Board of Regents, who was involved with strategic planning and policy analysis at Stanford Research Institute (SRI) at the time some joint projects were undertaken with the Institute for Noetic Sciences.

The paranormal emphasis that was Mitchell's has now shifted to three main thrusts: the mind in healing; exceptional capabilities, such as remote viewing; and the supraconscious as a factor in remarkable transformations of human beings.

Examination of these new thrusts shows that it retains the Institute's original "heresy." Whereas empirical science says the fundamental stuff of the universe is matter/energy, the Institute says it is consciousness.

IS THE "STUFF" OF THE
BACKSTER EFFECT CONSCIOUSNESS?

When Willis Harmon talks about "the deep inner sense of purpose in people, the power of the vision, the power of imagery, the power of affirmation"[1] it sounds as if he is talking about the Silva Mind Control, although he does not specifically mention it.

When Willis Harmon says, "We're trying to make the point that there's a wide range of exceptional mysterious abilities among plants and animals and humans,"[2] it sounds as if he is talking about the Backster Effect, although he does not specifically mention that either.

When he adds, "We will probably arrive at a better understanding if we study the whole spectrum than if we take one phenomenon," he is echoing this author's thrust in this book.

THE REAL BREAKTHROUGH: PSYCHOTRONICS

Consciousness has been conscious of itself for a long time. But only recently has consciousness become conscious that its source may not be limited to a three-pound organ called the brain, but may be interconnected with all individual consciousness and indeed to a larger consciousness.

Consciousness has an energy component. We do not fully understand this energy, but we do know that man has not created anything in this world without it first appearing as a mental image.

A clothing designer "sees" the garment, and sketches it. Then a pattern is made and the item can be manufactured. A piece of furniture is "seen" and sketched and machine drawings permit it to be manufactured. A building is "seen" first by the architect; then come sketches, renderings, plans, elevations, specifications, bids and finally construction.

Consciousness provides the energetic "seed" for creation. Back at that 1975 Monte Carlo Psychotronic Conference mentioned earlier in this chapter, the following definition was adopted for the word "psychotronics" by the scores of scientists in every discipline and both East and West:

Psychotronics

"The science which studies fields of interaction between people and their environment, internal and external, and the energetic processes involved. It recognizes that matter, energy, and consciousness are interconnected, which fact provides new understanding of the human body, of life processes, and of matter."

We have known that matter and energy are interconnected, but considering consciousness and energy as interconnected was a radical new concept not for practitioners in the new physics and in the new holistic approach to health, but for the adherents to the old paradigms of physics and medicine.

One of the greatest blows struck against such old paradigms was the inherent declaration that scientists (and physicians) were no longer able to consider themselves as objective observers. Their consciousness was affecting the outcome, whether they believed it was or not, and whether they wanted it to or not.

Psychotronics is the study of how brain neurons energetically affect body cells, other organic cells, and even inorganic matter.

At least one of the co-authors of *The Secret Life of Plants* was at that conference. Little wonder. Psychotronics was offering a scientific explanation of the Backster Effect about which he had written.

ARE SOVIET SCIENTISTS AHEAD OF THE U.S.?

The author delivered a paper at the Third World Psychotronic Conference in Tokyo in 1977. Many new faces were in evidence among Western scientists, especially from the United States, but Soviet Union scientists were conspicuously absent. Apparently, they found in Monte Carlo two years before that they had more to give than to receive.

According to Martin Ebon[3], who is not only a lifelong researcher/writer on Soviet affairs but a psychic researcher for over 25 years, it was about that time the Kremlin was clamping down on the publication of Soviet psychic research findings and contacts between parapsychologists and their Western counterparts were being discouraged.

The Soviet secret police – KGB – as well as the Ministry of Interior – MVD – was reported by Ebon to be keeping an eye on psychotronics particularly and especially on G.A. Samoyler, elected as the vice president for the Eastern Hemisphere at the first conference of the International Association for Psychotronic

Research held in Prague in 1973. It was at this conference that Cleve Backster served as Chairman of the "Interaction Between Man and Nature" section.

Judging from the powers of the mind which the author observed whether in person or on film in both Monte Carlo in 1975 and Tokyo in 1977, any major power working with psychotronics and its application in warfare would have as much reason to classify its psychotronics discoveries top secret as its electronics discoveries.

Changing the polarity of a magnetic field; moving objects across a table; detecting information at a distance and ahead in time – all with the energy of consciousness – have incipient military implications.

If these phenomena are associated in any way with an energy by whatever name that is related to primary perception, then the United States has an edge over other counties by having as one of its citizens a scientist named Cleve Backster.

IF WE KNEW HOW TO CONTROL
THE BACKSTER EFFECT...

It does not take a "science fiction" mentality to imagine the military advantages possible if we knew how to control the Backster Effect. Changing wrong attitudes at a distance, knowing intentions, detecting strategic information behind enemy lines, possibly even igniting inflammables and explosives. These are just the ones we can imagine here and now from square one. Even the sky is not the limit, so when we reach square one hundred and one, a world of differences may become a world of unity.

The secret life of cells would no longer be secret. The fact that cells, perhaps even inorganic molecules, are part of an infinite intelligence would be common knowledge. We would know that they know. Perhaps they would know that we knew.

We would also be able to tap that knowledge in order to manifest creative objectives anywhere in the universe – harnessing primary perception to communicate with colon cells to relieve constipation, or with atmospheric molecules to close the gap in the ozone layer.

In *Secret Life of Plants*, the authors report on the technical advances of Japanese scientists who have been able to zero in on plant to plant communication energy. One lunch break they left their apparatus pointing skyward and returned to find a read-out. On further exploration, they found several points in the heavens where communication at the plant level was recorded, leading to the possible conclusion that plants wherever they were in the universe are communicating with plants here.

In the Silva Mind Control training which leads to practical applications of primary perception in detecting health problems at a distance, some of the conditioning statements are: "I am now able to attune my intelligence by developing my sensing faculties and to project them to any point on this planet...any planet within the solar system, any solar system within the galaxy, any galaxy within the universe."

Although brain neurons respond to this conditioning in a dependable way for "any point on this planet," no opportunities have been presented for such use in other planets, solar systems or galaxies. Assuming that this is a right brain function and knowing of the right brains ability to function in a pre-creation realm that is not limited by post-creation's time and space, it is not unreasonable to expect that brain neurons' primary perception can be limitless.

Perhaps the Silva Mind Control training is one way of getting in control of the Backster Effect.

THE ROLE OF THE BRAIN'S RIGHT HEMISPHERE

Certainly the Silva Method is one way of getting in control of more of your mind, especially the right hemisphere. As discussed previously, right brain research points to it being a factor in connecting us to Jung's collective unconscious or that field of consciousness Edgar Mitchell hypothesizes permeates the universe and which Rupert Sheldrake calls the morphogenetic field on a more localized scale.

Call it what you may, the right brain must therefore be a prime factor in the Backster Effect, at least as it is manifested by human cells.

Because the right brain is oriented to unity as opposed to polarity or dichotomy which is the interest of the left brain, many believe that it is the right brain that connects us to where we came from. That is, the energy source of matter – creative energy – is the right brain realm while the polarization of that creative energy into the positive nucleus and negative electrons of the atom is the left brain realm.

One comes before two. So, right brain is in the causal or creative realm, left brain the effect or material realm. Science or religion, which have been at each other's throats for centuries, find themselves as bedfellows in this concept. At least it points to there being a spiritual basis behind the physical world.

It helps to explain the Chinese Qi or Chi, a measurable physical force emitted by masters at will, and its Japanese counterpart KI demonstrated in the martial arts. It is the healing energy behind physical illness harnessed by the Silva Method and other holistic approaches to healing now being hailed in scores of books being published on the subject. It is psychotronic energy.

At a recent California conclave of doctors in Los Angeles, sponsored by the American Medical Association, the American Hospital Association, and the Association of Medical Colleges, it was agreed that as credible alternative therapies emerge, a revised relationship of physicians and their patients may emerge, reversing the current trend to protect the medical corporation first at the expense of the medical principle to protect the patient.

If we are to function with both sides of our brain, what better area for this bicameral mind to begin than health care.

THE BACKSTER EFFECT AS A WINDOW INTO...

In December 1985, the *International Journal of Biosocial Research*[4] published a paper by Cleve Backster and Stephen G. White entitled, "Biocommunications Capability: Human Donors and In Vitro Leukocytes."

Covered in the paper are 12 examples of these mouth cells reacting at a distance to emotional arousal in the donor – all illustrated by a graphic read-out of the EEG-type instrumentation.

With typical Backster conservatism the paper concludes that further "research into this biocommunication phenomenon could possibly lead to new avenues of knowledge concerning genetics, immunology, the healing process and the mind-brain relationship."

Giving credit to a more far-reaching supposition, the authors also mention the possibility of a new energy being involved and the possible value of monitoring in vitro white cells at considerable earth distances from their donor. "Should there be meaningful observations at such distances, the same technology, with the addition of telemetry, would be justifiable as part of a space probe to determine possible attenuation effect and time consumption of the signal."

This places the paper's authors at the approximate center of opinion as to the philosophical and scientific implications of the Backster Effect, with most scientists preferring not to have to confront it at all, and others seeing it as a major breakthrough.

It is reminiscent of the old fable about the blind men's first experience with an elephant (so old that the author's memory of it requires the taking of liberties.) The blind man feeling the trunk said the elephant is like a snake. The one feeling the ears said the elephant is like a flying bat. The one feeling the tusk said the elephant is like a warrior.

It must be said that the lay person sees the Backster Effect as a confirmation of telepathy at the cell level.

The scientist sees the Backster Effect as a phenomenon that does not fit existing scientific parameters.

The philosopher sees the Backster Effect as a primary perception affording a window into the secrets of the universe.

The spiritual leader sees the Backster Effect as the possible scientific discovery of God.

––––––––––––––

Footnotes:

[1]*The New Heresy*, Steve Diamond, The American Theosophist, Spring, 1987

[2]*Ibid*

[3]*Psychic Warfare: Threat or Illusion?*, Martin Ebon, McGraw-Hill, 1983

[4]Volume 7, No. 2, Publication Office: P.O. Box 1174, Tacoma, WA 98401-1174

Chapter VIII

Supportive Theories
From Jung To Sheldrake

Politics is a sinister activity. Albeit necessary to democracy, its tendency to hit below the belt, crucify, and denigrate lowers the very people it strives to elevate.

Politics exists in the ranks of scientists. They are quick to hurl epithets, claim fraud, and ridicule opponents, all of which boomerangs, rendering them unscientific.

Just as an occasional statesman appears on the political horizon, a scientist of stature occasionally rises above the politics of science.

In this chapter, we will cover the work of several of these scientists, especially as to how their findings and hypotheses contribute to a broader understanding of the Backster Effect and its implications.

To better appreciate the contrast, the author would like to take the reader through the muck and mire first so that the illumination of these statesmen and philosophers of science can be better appreciated.

A common tactic of the critics of metaphysics or parapsychology is to lump these approaches with astrology, out-of-body experiences, the Bermuda Triangle, UFOs and any other approaches they consider suspect which actually proves nothing but their own intellectual snobbery.

A pet argument that has surfaced a number of times in the past several decades has been: Even when fraud cannot be found, it is more logical to believe it exists than to conclude that the laws of nature have been violated.

Critics insist that magicians not scientists investigate paranormal demonstrations. They use the word pseudoscience meaning it is something that claims to be science but is not. They say that science takes the mystery out of things, so if mystery is the result of a demonstration, such as remote viewing, it is then not science.

One of the most vitriolic crusade's against parapsychology has been waged by *The Humanist*, the official organ of the American Humanist Association. Some of their special issues have been "Antiscience and Pseudoscience," "The New Cults," and "The Psychics Debunked."

These and others warn of apocalyptic consequences, society run amok, and revenge by Higher Authority if researchers in the Rhine and Backster genre are not suppressed.

Personal defamation is a favorite tool. In discussing the remote viewing work of Russell Targ and Harold Puthoff at SRI, one of these articles said, "Targ's father at one time owned a bookstore that sold nut books on everything from phrenology to hypnotism and astrology. So Targ is fundamentally a believer in these things." And this, "Dr. Puthoff is a scientologist. I hardly need to mention to you the abandonment of reasoning powers this would indicate."

These are scientists talking as if they were the spokespeople for the profession. If they are, God help the profession. Oops. An unscientific phrase.

It is natural that new ideas are resisted. But there should be no resistance to the testing of new ideas using the scientific process.

However, propose such tests to expand the present frontiers into the powers of consciousness and life energy and you are labeled as believing in ouija boards, God and the devil.

"IT DID NOT WORK FOR ME,
SO IT DOES NOT EXIST"

One leading critic of ESP explained his position this way: If the choice is between believing in something radically contradictory to contemporary thought or believing in fraud and self-delusion, which is more reasonable? A paraphrasing of their pet argument.

One scientist publicly criticized Backster by saying, "He is not a trained scientist." He suggested that Backster's instruments were providing him with "noise" rather than true signals.

This was not only pointing to the fact that Backster does not have a Ph.D. but it was also saying that he was not competent with the equipment. Of course, this is absurd. The equipment used then was the modified Stoelting polygraph, using a technology that Backster had by that time worked with for 27 years. There was nobody as competent as he was. This critic was either vindictively or unprofessionally ignoring Backster's long service as chairman of the Research and Instrument Committee of the Academy for Scientific Interrogation; his service as director and Research Chairman of the American Polygraph Association; and his having been called upon by Congress twice as an expert witness as to the limitations and capabilities of this lie detecting instrumentation.

The brunt of attacks against the Backster Effect has come from those who were disappointed by their failure to replicate it. But they failed because they did not faithfully follow the recommended procedures, deeming them extraneous or non-critical to the outcome.

"It does not exist" is their inevitable claim, in one stroke saving their own face and besmirching Backster's.

Backster summarizes the usual causes of these failures as follows:

1. Graduate students working under pressure to meet deadlines are not psychologically attuned to obtaining results in the area of consciousness research.

2. When experiments are carried out during the day (his are done largely late at night,) and in the normal environment of the busy biological laboratory, stimuli from the whole building can cause biological "noise" making it unlikely that plants would

respond to a particular experimental stimulus.

3. Changes were made like increasing the number of brine shrimp "drops." Plants show an adaptation effect which dilutes the data. Another change, changing from a D.C. to A.C. instrumentation circuit might also cause failure but this is not thoroughly understood. In situations where an attunement to consciousness may be involved, we had best not jump arbitrarily from one technique to another.

4. Relationships between experimenter and plants were not carefully controlled in the appropriate manner before the experiments. (Can you imagine scientists being conscientious about their plants' "attachment" or lack thereof?)

5. The monitoring equipment was set for automatic recentering which eliminates certain data and disturbs the outcome.

The scientific frame of mind which says, "If I can't replicate it, it cannot be replicated" is presumptuous and pompous. It goes by the old school that considers a scientist as an impartial observer of the research he is doing.

The opposite is now known to be true. Every scientist is a factor in the experiment.

CONSCIOUSNESS BEGINS TO
MAKE ITS MARK

Now, let's look at the light at the end of the tunnel.

In the past few years, the United States Food and Drug Administration has issued over 150 researching licenses to investigate the possible uses of the Voll Machine, also called the Dermatron, and Electroacupuncture According to Voll (EAV).

The originator of this system is a German physician, Dr. Reinhard Voll. With the Voll Machine, the physician presses one electrode against the patients acupoint suspected of being involved with the health problem, while the patient holds the other electrode thus completing an electric circuit. The resulting difference of potential then appears on the machine's voltmeter. This is compared to a list of normal readings.

An acupoint reading that is lower than normal can be caused by a degenerative disease. One that is higher than normal can be caused by some inflammation. The machine can be switched to treatment and voltage charges delivered to the acupoint which is connected to a larger meridian or energy circuit of the body. The ability of this meridian to accept and retain the charge provides more diagnostic information about the illness.

The next step in the use of the Voll Machine is "where the action is." When a small circular stand, containing holes to accommodate medicinal samples, is attached to the Voll Machine, any substance placed in one of these holes becomes part of the energy circuit and affects the read-out. The physician can then test different remedies to see which restores a normal read-out. This opens up a vast field for identifying the cause of allergic responses and taking corrective action.

Despite its history of success, the Voll Machine has conventional physicians stroking their chins and more likely than not, turning away and toward more hit-and-miss approaches.

The Voll Machine is still the most accepted among the acupoint-meridian based electronic diagnosis systems. More sophisticated ones have been and are being developed.

What goes even beyond these electrically-oriented devices is the radionic system. It seldom uses electricity but depends on the consciousness energy of the practitioner. Because of this it is more accurately termed to be a psychotronic, not electronic, device.

Sometimes called the "black box," it depends on the psychic abilities of the practitioner. The device's operator must have a consciousness of expectation and belief in the system. This attunement enables him or her to obtain a large amount of valuable diagnostic material from even one drop of the patient's blood.

Called the "witness," this small piece of the whole body contains within it the total energetic structure of the donor body – its dynamic frequency spectrum. More about this feature when we discuss holographic principles.

Far out? Well, these radionic systems have proven to be effective tools, in spite of gaps in the understanding of how they work even with those who use them, and certainly with scientific critics.

Picture the scene. The radionic operator is seated by the black box. He or she places a lock of hair or spot of blood into a small circular metallic well. Next is added a piece of paper with the client's name. The operator begins to think of the patient and gently strokes a rubber pad connected by an insulated wire to the black box. Simultaneously , using the other hand, the operator turns the first of several dials on the front of the black box.

The operator feels a response on the rubber pad. It is a sticking sensation. The second dial is then turned until this same response is felt again. Once all the dials have been adjusted, they combine to produce a number which reflects the energy characteristics of the client who could be miles away, and to this energy factor is coupled by past experience the nature of the problem.

What a field day this can provide for the critics! However, the critics have either not taken this seriously enough, or they are giving it the same silent treatment that they once gave the Backster Effect, in the hopes that it will go away.

This is an example of the microcosm of research parallel to primary perception that is going to have to be reckoned with one day by scientists. They cannot go on forever sweeping unexplained phenomena such as this under the bed.

The voice of consciousness is beginning to be heard.

CONSCIOUSNESS INCREASES IN OUR UNDERSTANDING OF THE UNIVERSE

When, early in this century, the prime minister of South Africa, a Boer general named Jan Christian Smuts, wrote in his "Holism and Evolution" about a strong unifying principle that was organizing nature, he was describing a growing consciousness in the universe.

In the late 1920's, the Greek novelist Nikos Kazantzakis called God the evolutionary drive of consciousness in the universe.

In the next decade, Pierre Teilhard de Chardin was proclaiming the advent of a greater awareness which he called "the cumulative ardor of the collective soul."

But it was Carl Jung, the Swiss psychoanalyst, who introduced the concept of a larger consciousness in which each person shared – the collective unconscious – and was able to document its existence with common dream symbols and synchronicity which pointed to a racial memory or superconscious.

Jung's teachings are coming of age. Books on his work are selling more than ever before. Consciousness is beginning to become conscious of itself.

As it does, consciousness sees itself reflected in all of the universe. To understand the new physics, to understand their own intuitive and creative abilities, to explain what they see in the laboratory, philosopher-scientists are forced into accepting the concept of a larger intelligence filling all space.

In a moment we will discuss the proof of the existence of Jung's collective unconscious, albeit with some new terminology. But, first it is interesting to see how die-hard scientists leap-frog over these findings in order to maintain their "party" line.

Writing in the American Museum of Natural History magazine *Natural History*, the consummate critic Arthur W. Galston says of Peter Tompkins and Christopher Bird, authors of *The Secret Life of Plants*:

"How can any two reasonable authors advance so many patently false, unprovable, or impossible conclusions? The answer is by ignoring all the ordinary rules of evidence and by damning, circumventing, or flouting the scientific method whenever it serves their purpose to do so."

What Galston is ignoring is the fact that what he calls "the rules of evidence" are beginning to evolve in the direction of consciousness being a key factor. This is developing even in experiments that seem not to include consciousness in their scope.

IS THERE A UNITY BEHIND ALL LIFE?

"The purpose of life is to evolve consciousness until it becomes one with the light which created it. To witness this light, this invisible light of consciousness, is to see the glory of all the suns and stars inside one small microscopic cell of the human brain."

This quote is from *Nuclear Evolution*[1] by Dr. Christopher Hills, one of the country's leading researchers in the field of consciousness and radionics. Hills sees every major scientific discovery as a new way of looking at nature, requiring the looker to leave familiar concepts behind. "The ultimate science is nature," he says, "and the ultimate scientist is the cosmic intelligence."

Hills epitomized the communicator of a new planetary consciousness which Marilyn Ferguson calls "The Aquarian Conspiracy."

She points out that when Einstein's theory of relativity displaced Newton's physics, old timers received the new paradigms with mockery and hostility. They reacted again as they did with Copernicus, Pasteur and Mesmer. It took a new generation to recognize the power of the new understanding.

Historian and philosopher Thomas Kuhn pointed out in the 1960's that scientists who were successful working within the old paradigms rarely if ever are converted. They are so emotionally attached that even when confronted with overwhelming evidence they stick with the wrong but familiar precepts and eventually go to their grave with them.

This is a dismal picture of the scientist. But it is changing. As Richard Gerber, M.D., states in *Vibrational Medicine*, human consciousness is learning, growing and evolving. "As spiritual awareness of this dynamic process of change becomes more prevalent, there will be a ripple effect that will shift the energetic dynamics of the human race as a whole."

Look around. That ripple effect has already begun.

New thought religions are proliferating, their central theme being that we are part of a larger intelligence that permeates the universe. New approaches in business are beginning to give cooperation priority over competition. Philosophers and scientists are beginning to hypothesize that space is not nothingness but something – a continuum with such properties as awareness and intelligence.

Meanwhile, at a lab in San Diego, Backster and White have extracted leukocytes from the mouth of a 32-year-old divorced woman, and have readied the monitoring equipment with her seated some five meters away.

At Backster's suggestion, she is talking about her youth.

"I had a dog named Duke," she reminisces.

Backster interrupts, "Isn't your step-son also named Duke?"

There is an immediate reaction by her mouth's white cells, as she displays unmistakable signs of emotion herself. (See Figure 6). A minute later, a question relating to the present well-being of her step-son triggers a similar reaction by her white cells. A recent divorce had separated her from this step-son whom she had raised.

If this is microcosm of a new awareness of consciousness as filling all space, it fits the macrocosm.

THE SCIENTIFIC CONCEPT
OF A LARGER INTELLIGENCE

When Dr. Rupert Sheldrake and neurologist Steven Rose debated Sheldrake's theory of a field of intelligence on the pages of the Manchester *Guardian* in Great Britain, a reader wrote the paper, "The truth probably is that we are all part of a universal intelligence just as bees are part of the 'hive-mind.'"[2]

This concept of a "hive-mind" can be seen in nature again and again. Salmon fighting their way up a river in the Pacific northwest to spawn and die. Not one salmon or a school of salmon, but maybe a million salmon, leave their salt water environment and brave climbing fresh water rapids.

Pigeons released from their cages atop a roof, fly together in widening circles, swooping and diving together as one.

The golden plover is born in Alaska and a few weeks later flies unerringly to Hawaii, singly, but in the thousands.

Ants cooperate in such dramatic ways that we call them a social insect. A species of African termite is blind. It builds a towering nest. A second such nest is built by a nearby group. At precisely the same height, each group tilts it toward the other creating a perfect arch!

Monkeys were observed on islands off Japan to shun sweet potatoes even though food was scarce. When one monkey on one side of one of the islands taught another to wash the sweet potato off in the ocean, break it open, and eat it, and when about one hundred monkeys began to enjoy the sweet potatoes, in a flash all the monkeys on that island and nearby islands began eating the sweet potatoes.

Are there no examples of humans behaving as if they shared a higher intelligence? There is no definitive proof of this in cults, trends and fads, nor was there in Hitler's hysteria or the hopes of communism.

But there is now, thanks to Dr. Rupert Sheldrake, on the planetary scale and hopefully support for it on the local scale as the Backster Effect and certain individual capabilities.

The latter might include Uri Geller's talents, such as erasing a computer image, and the ability of some people to cause frequent failures in computers.

Sheldrake sees a field of computer-like intelligence activating and being activated by every form of life. Morphic fields, as he calls them, resonate with other morphic fields. So, not only do we all gain from each other, but if we are like some other species of life we can benefit through morphic resonance.

Attempted demonstrations have been eminently successful. Rats learn a maze and after that their brothers and sisters learn it faster. People can memorize an old nursery rhyme in a foreign language faster than a modern one. Students, tested with words of a foreign language interspersed with fake words, are able to sense which are genuine.

When Sheldrake's first book was published (*A New Science of Life*, Jeremy P. Tarcher, 1981), one reviewer called it "the best candidate for burning" in many years.

It certainly provides an earthquake of about eight on the Richter scale for Newtonian thinkers who are still chopping up nature into its smallest possible units.

At the same time it is a fortuitous synchronicity to the Backsters of the world.

CONSCIOUSNESS WITH A SMALL "c"; CONSCIOUSNESS WITH A LARGE "C"

Computer specialists see a parallel in Sheldrake's hypothesis and their own activities. Small computers can plug into larger computers, as through telephone lines, giving them access to larger bodies of data than those with which they have been programmed.

Can the consciousness of a human being, itself with computer-like capabilities tap into a larger computer, a higher field of consciousness, inferred by Sheldrake's work?

Space is filled with consciousness and/or intelligence; your cells occupy space; your cells are filled with consciousness and/or intelligence.

Reasonable? Or, non-sequitur?

If you say non-sequitur, you are a product of the Newtonian Age Thinking. If you say reasonable, you are one step beyond.

If it is reasonable that cells and organisms have access to the intelligence that fills all space, the Backster Effect is no mystery. Neither is remote viewing, Silva Mind Control, absent healing, or out-of-body (O.O.B.) experiences.

All three are the projecting of individual intelligence into the collective intelligence – consciousness with a small "c" into Consciousness with a capital "C."

The O.O.B. is perhaps the most unique of these three approaches. The ones who experience this phenomenon appear to be able to travel in space. They appear to be able to see their own physical body where they left it. It has been reported throughout history in many cultures, including Greeks and Egyptians. It is mentioned by St. Paul in I Corinthians and by such writers as D.H. Lawrence, Jack London, and Aldous Huxley.

In 1971, the Monroe Institute of Applied Sciences opened to explore expanded states of human consciousness, especially the O.O.B. Its founder was Robert Monroe, a former vice president in charge of programming for the Mutual Broadcasting system and owner of a number of radio stations and cable TV stations.

In 1958, Monroe began to have O.O.B. experiences. At first he thought he was deranged or had a brain tumor. His doctor offered only tranquilizers. He decided he must either be sedated the rest of his life or get in control of the out-of-body state. He chose the latter.

O.O.B. became his life interest and remained so for three decades and the institute eventually attracted scores of serious researchers to join him in the pursuit of understanding this phenomenon.

Monroe began experimenting with brain synchronizers and resonators that he could use to help others to control their mental states. He developed a sound that triggered a sort of body-asleep-mind-awake state that caused a number of O.O.B. experiences albeit different from his own.

It was at this point that he founded the Institute in Virginia and began offering a seven-day training that was called the "Gateway Voyage." Thousands have now taken this training. They include people in all walks of life with the professions well represented--one scientist being Rupert Sheldrake.

Monroe's own O.O.B experiences sound like they were out of "Arabian Nights" – places where space and time do not exist, where communication is by thought transference, and where zombies moved about. Graduates of the training claim benefits that relate more to effectiveness in this material world than to any other O.O.B. realms – a broadening of perspective.

THE FUNCTION OF THE RIGHT BRAIN
IN CONNECTING THE INDIVIDUAL PERSON
TO THE WHOLE

When the Maimonides Dream Laboratory was doing its land-mark work in the 1960's as a project of the Maimonides Medical Center in Brooklyn, psychologist Dr. Stanley Krippner was able to have a sender in a room 100 feet away choose a picture at random and influence the dreams of a sleeping subject.

The sender might have chosen "The Last Supper" by Da Vinci. He stared at it. The sleeper was monitored by both the brain encephalograph that measures brain wave frequencies and a muscle movement detector attached to the eyes.

When the observer saw the movement detector register rapid eye movement (REM), which indicates dreaming, the sleeping subject was awakened and asked what he was dreaming about.

"It was a dream about a big dinner. There were a lot of men at the table."

In one actual case, a young secretary volunteered to be the sleeper. A psychologist doing the sending chose Gaugin's "The Moon and the Earth" which depicts a Tahitian girl in the nude. In the dream that resulted, the secretary said she was in a bathing suit, saw a clothesline she could hang it on and felt the need to get a suntan.

What the researchers at the Dream Laboratory were not as familiar with then as they would in all likelihood be today was the role in this phenomenon that the right hemisphere of the brain played.

The right hemisphere is recessive, the left dominant in the active, awake state. When you relax deeply, brain waves slow up and the two hemispheres tend to come into balance. This is called the alpha state.

Asleep, your brain waves are even slower than the alpha state, except when you dream. Dreaming is at the alpha state. So it involves the right brain hemisphere.

In a moment, we will look at the job description of the right brain hemisphere. But first a reminder.

The Backster Effect is a response of your cells to your feelings. Feelings are a right brain function. The right brain is your connection to the creative realm. The creative realm is the source of this field of consciousness. Conclusion: Because they are in tune with the consciousness that fills all space, your cells are in tune with your consciousness at all times no matter where they are in your body – or out.

In the final chapter, we will review how you can train yourself to go to the alpha level, activate your right hemisphere so as to be able to obtain creative solutions to problems, and to detect and correct health problems, summarizing the successful procedures now in use.

"Miracles" result. They are the equivalent of miracles unless you understand the awesome ability of every cell of your body to tap into intelligence – yours and the universe's. You can keep no secret from your body's cells.

THE TWO HEMISPHERES OF OUR BRAIN AND THEIR SEPARATE RESPONSIBILITIES

Up until a few decades ago, all we really knew about the two hemispheres of the human brain was that the left hemisphere ran the right side of the body and the right hemisphere ran the left side of the body. Also, we knew that if one hemisphere was damaged, the other would come to its rescue as a sort of back-up system.

When the medical profession began to separate these two halves of the brain as a way of relieving certain brain-related conditions – the lobotomy – they were able to begin to see a difference in the way these two hemispheres functioned. This was not possible before, because the two hemispheres have as many connectors interchanging information as there are telephones on earth.

However, these experiments were on abnormal brains and could not be properly assumed to be applied to normal brains.

It was not until they began to work with an anesthetic – amelobarbitone being the most useful – injecting it into one blood vessel to "knock out" the right hemisphere, another to "knock out" the other hemisphere, that a definitive, generally applicable, understanding of the separate functions of these two hemispheres emerged.

Summarizing the main characteristics of left brain and right brain thinking:

* The left brain is interested in the objective, physical world. The right brain is more interested in the subjective non-physical world, the world of emotion and feelings, the world of visualization and imagination.

* The left brain is interested in physical activity, body motion.

The right brain turns toward passivity – musing, meditation, mental picturing.

   * The left brain thinks logically, linearly. The right brain is more spatial in its approach, and goes more by gut feeling.

   * The left brain thrives on detail. It is down to earth in its point of view. The right brain sees the whole picture. It has the bird's-eye point of view.

   * The left brain is attracted by conflict, polarity, dichotomy. The right brain sees the common denominators, the agreements, the unity behind the polarity.

The unity behind polarity. The oneness behind the twoness. The Einstein not the Newton.

A relative of Albert Einstein visited the headquarters of the Theosophical Society in America shortly after his death. She wanted to tell the people there that Einstein always kept his desk clear of papers, charts, and other paraphernalia that cluttered the desks of most scientists. There was one exception: a book entitled *The Secret Doctrine* by Blavatsky, the founder of Theosophy.

The gist of that secret doctrine which is behind theosophical approaches is that we are not separate units of intelligence but part of a larger intelligence that unites all humankind.

This is the way the right brain sees things – oneness.

The left brain sees things differently – twoness.

Which brain is correct?

YOU ARE A BRIDGE BETWEEN TWO REALMS

Both hemispheres are correct.

The left brain is interested in this physical world. It senses what we need to survive in it. Our education is largely left-brained so we can work in this physical world.

The physical world is a twoness. The atom is the division of energy into plus and minus. The plus is the nucleus of the atom, the minus is the electrons rotating around the nucleus.

Which comes first: one or two? One. So the non-physical world, the realm of the right hemisphere, would have to be the causal realm, with the physical realm the effect.

So, having a left and a right hemisphere, one attuned to the effect, the other to the cause makes us a bridge between where we came from and where we are now.

The physical world is the Newtonian world of building blocks of matter. The causal realm is the energy world from which matter crystallized. Smash the atom and it returns to its element-- energy, where Newtonian thinking (left brain) ends and Einstein- ian thinking (right brain) begins.

Can you begin to see why the Randis and Galstons think the way they do? Can you blame them? Of course not. From their physical point of view, the non-physical cannot exist.

Can you begin to see why the Sheldrakes and Backsters think the way they do? From what they see, the non-physical is to be seriously reckoned with.

ENTER THE SILVA METHOD–
A WAY TO CROSS THE BRIDGE

Peek into this hotel room.

A lecturer is reading from a large manual. The audience is an average cross-section of the local populace, young and old, black and white, lay and professional. However, there is one thing unique about them: they are listening with their eyes closed.

As you watch, occasionally they raise their hands in unison as if they were reaching out for an object, or knocking on a door, or manipulating something.

These people are taking a four-day training called the Silva Mind Control Method. Its purpose is to change their thinking from left brain dominated to both brain balanced. From eccentric to centered.

Why spend four valuable days and hundreds of dollars to activate the right brain? Because you become connected to the larger computer, the higher intelligence, the universal conscious- ness or whatever else you may want to call the oneness that is the creative realm, creating the twoness we call the physical realm.

Why seek that connection? Silva graduates answer that question starting with the first day of training. After learning how to go to the relaxed alpha level, they are able to program themselves to fall asleep at will, wake up at a precise time without an alarm clock, stay awake when fatigued on the job, end headaches, and order a dream that contains information to help solve some up until then insoluble problem.

They continue to learn how to use their connection to this creative realm on the next day by discovering they have a fantastic memory using the right hemisphere--remembering not by rote but by amusing mental picturing. They program a simple triggering device – putting three fingers together – which activates more of the mind. Changing problem oriented thinking to solution oriented thinking, getting rid of pain anywhere in the body, programming water to help with the solution to a problem, and programming away unwanted behavior such as smoking and over-eating is the ground covered the second day.

Each student thus far has acquired mental "tools" to use the rest of his or her life. But that's just the beginning.

What happens at the end of the third and fourth days of training gives even right-brainers goose bumps.

During these two days, the training exercises are aimed at providing the right hemisphere with the points of reference that the left hemisphere has acquired in physical world experiences but of which the right brain, because of its lack of usage is devoid.

Once accomplished, the graduates are able to demonstrate to themselves and others that they can function mentally in a way that transcends physical limitations of time and space. They are connected via the right hemisphere to that very space-filling intelligence that the Jungs, Sheldrakes and Backsters are proclaiming.

Their intuition is dependable. Their guessing is accurate. Their problem-solving ability is awesome. But perhaps even more important: They are in touch with their body's cells and even the cells of other bodies, though they be thousands of miles away.

This mind-to-cell contact makes the detection of abnormalities such as sickness and disease a simple matter of going to the alpha level through relaxation and mentally asking to "see" the problem. Their mind is attracted to the area of the problem.

Not that we have shifted from using the word "brain" to using the word "mind." This is because by activating the right hemisphere, we may actually be using the intelligence or consciousness that fills all space. It appears to be that we are projecting our own intelligence, but that may well be a left brain way of looking at it, when actually we may be tapping into a left brain unmentionable,--a field of intelligence that we all share.

Jose Silva, the founder of this training, researched it for 22 years before going public with it in 1966. He lived in Laredo, Texas, at the same location where the world-wide headquarters of the organization is still located, serving over eight million graduates, and hundreds of lecturers in some 50 countries. In the past 22 years of growth, it has spawned scores of imitators and copyright infringements, most of which are no longer around.

More important, it gave rise to a new branch of medicine called psychoneuroimmunology.

What is it?

YOU CAN "TALK" TO YOUR BODY'S CELLS AND THEY GET THE MESSAGE

The late philosopher Joseph Campbell saw in all the myths of the world's cultures a single fundamental myth. The imaginary (right brain) tales were tapping into the same source of wisdom and proclaiming a unifying intelligence despite race or geographical location.

When you relax, go to the alpha level and thus activate the right brain, you are enhancing your connection to that continuum of intelligence that fills all space. You are plugged into what appears to function as a huge switch board.

Picture somebody and your brain neurons are plugged into theirs. You never get a wrong number. Picture that person's kidney and the psychotronic energy of your consciousness is in tune with that person's energy body. If you see a stone in that kidney, crush it in your imagination, "see" it dissolving in the urine. Let your final mental picture be of a perfect kidney free of stones. And it becomes so.

Telephone your friend and expect, "Hey, that stone in my kidney — I just passed it."

Can you contact the cells of your own body? A resounding yes. When you put in a call to your immune system cells and goad them on to repel an invader you are using psychoneuroimmunology.

The medical profession is still wrestling with that one but physicians such as Irving Oyle, Carl Simonton, Bernie Siegel, and Richard Gerber are pacesetters and the author apologizes to the hundreds more who have seen the potential for having their patients help them in the healing process.

To a less intense degree, many other physicians and psychologists are using the same principles. They are encouraging mental sets of cure and recovery even in what they would otherwise call "terminal" cases. The result: unexplained remissions.

Positive mind sets are creative. They create the solution. Where the problem is one of health, they tend to create cure.

Negative mind sets are destructive. They reinforce the problem. They continue the illness.

Significant bio-energetic principles are being conceived by humanity. Backster is but one channel for this of many. This is resulting in the appearance of an "Einsteinian" approach to healing.

Your brain neurons communicate with your body cells, via the creative realm.

You fix yourself up. You stay well.

Footnotes:

[1]University of the Trees Press, Boulder Creek, California, 1972

[2]excerpted from *Brain/Mind Bulletin*, Volume 13, No. 11, August, 1988

Chapter IX

Needed: A New Scientific Method

In these final two chapters we have two important messages to deliver.

The first is a message to the professional world of scientific researchers. The second is a message to you.

The first message: changes must be made in certain research approaches to enable the occult life of cells to be de-occulted so that a new science of consciousness can arise to benefit humankind. It is the topic of this chapter.

The second message: here is how you the reader can contact your cells and affect their life for the benefit of your life. These how-to instructions for better health are in the final chapter.

First, humanity demands a new scientific method where consciousness is involved.

At the present writing, two-time Nobel laureate Linus C. Pauling is 87. He still heads the Linus Pauling Institute of Science and Medicine in Palo Alto, California where 50 people, 20 of whom have doctorates, work to get his vitamin C findings accepted. The Institute, which he founded in 1973, draws over $3 million a year in funding largely from private sources.

Still, his contention that vitamin C can deter the common cold, work against cancer and AIDS, and raise the I.Q. of mentally retarded children by as much as 20 points, has not been accepted by mainstream physicians.

"We know of no evidence..." etc. etc. Of course, they don't, because when that evidence is presented, they refuse to accept it and turn away.

In theory, science is open to new ideas.

In practice, science is open to new sources of funding. Period. Foundations and government agencies are the target. These funders follow safe guidelines based on past rather than innovative research methods. Stick to the tried and true and you get the grant. Innovate and you get the gate.

Pauling has done better than most scientific frontiersmen. Researchers like Backster and Pauling must depend on private individuals whose purse strings are not controlled by vested interests protecting the status quo, but who want to play a role in humanity's progress and well-being. They are the statesmen in financing.

Backster has certain projects on hold for lack of funds that, when initiated, could startle even the new energy-oriented physicists and electrically-oriented biologists.

What is really needed is a new understanding about the intelligent universe which would render nothing startling. Then a scientist, using intelligent procedures, could explore the universe without being labeled a pseudoscientist.

An article appeared about Carl Sagan in the June, 1988 issue of the in-flight magazine *Vis àVis*. It said he used "the ironic wit of a satirist to wage a passionate campaign against pseudoscience." To this a retired army general replied in the November issue that Sagan himself was a pseudoscientist because of his nuclear winter thesis.

"Pseudo-" is in the eye of the beholder.

THE ONLY CONSTANT IS CHANGE

When custom controls the pursuit of knowledge, its chains inhibit progress. Hopefully, the chains of custom now restricting research into consciousness are reaching the breaking point.

One author who has added stress to those chains is David Berlinski who has taught philosophy and mathematics at universities in France and the United States. In *Black Mischief: The*

Mechanics of Modern Science[1], he shows how most of modern science is based on the outmoded Newtonian view of a mechanistic world.

Reciting his personal experience in the laboratories and seminar rooms of contemporary science, Berlinski holds a mirror up for all to see and it is not a pretty sight. Instead of a picture of impeccable integrity, sound reasoning, and unstoppable progress, we see a picture of personalities and prejudices rampant on a field of grant scrambling.

We Americans, who still feel a classical confidence in science as the ultimate source of progress, cannot even turn to Congress for help. They have already investigated the problem and thrown up their hands.

There was a feeling among some members of Congress that the research community had been lax in their efforts to curb fraud and unethical conduct. Two influential House members: John Dingell, Democrat of Michigan, and Henry Waxman, Democrat of California, drafted a measure in 1988 that was intended to create an office on science misconduct. The opposition by professional groups was immediate and immense. How could a federal agency do a better job in identifying misconduct, they insisted.

One Congressional aide, evaluating this flak, was quoted as saying, "What you're hearing are the screams of an industry about to be regulated for the first time."

It hangs in the balance whether there will be a follow-up by Congress or a follow-through by the research community.

One or the other must come.

PERSONAL EXPERIENCE: TRUE OR FALSE?

The author has been talking to the cells of his body for more than three decades. He started doing so when his study of Cosmo-Theosophy indicated it was possible. Further theosophical studies and practices in metaphysics, hypnosis, and psychotronics made his talking to the cells, organs and tissues of his body even more natural and productive.

When in the Fall of 1988, his leukocytes were extracted, centrifuged, and electrically monitored by Steve White and Cleve Backster in their San Diego laboratory, the first thing the author did when the read-out started was to mentally send love to those white cells no longer in his mouth but in a test tube about ten feet away. There was an immediate spike on the read-out chart.

Continued feelings of loving support yielded only squiggles.

Next, the author pulled out a breath sweetener from his pocket and decided to use it. Instantly there was a two-inch sweep of the pen that nearly went off the chart. Apparently, Binaca is a powerful germ killer for which the mouth's white cells had a great deal of respect. (See Figure 6).

There followed about an hour of leisurely conversation with our collective eyes on the televised read-out of white cell reactions. There were plenty. Every few minutes we said something that caused the author's mouth cells, now 15 feet away, to react. Among the topics that caused these reactions were subjective communication, the publishing business, and the healing abilities attained through the Silva Method. Once, Backster's cat Sam jumped up on the author's lap and the needle went crazy. Other times the cells appeared to react to what Backster was saying, but it also could be to what the author was hearing.

The author was completely comfortable with the experience. He has been "involved" in consciousness research for many years.

But what is the reaction of the man in the street?

"It's weird."

"Crazy, man."

"How is that possible?"

And what is the reaction of the conventional scientist?

"There is no control group."

"There is no standard protocol."

"There is no insulating of the equipment against outside interferences."

When the truth is unaccepted by others you take the critical consequences.

Shape up, Mr. Consciousness Researcher. Keep your findings within the bounds of the past, i.e. intelligible.

ACTION AT A DISTANCE
CHALLENGES INTELLIGIBILITY

Remote viewing is action at a distance.

Psychic functioning is action at a distance.

Absent healing is action at a distance.

So is the Backster Effect – action at a distance.

Action at a distance has always been a repugnant concept to scientists. The quantum theory has forced some reluctant

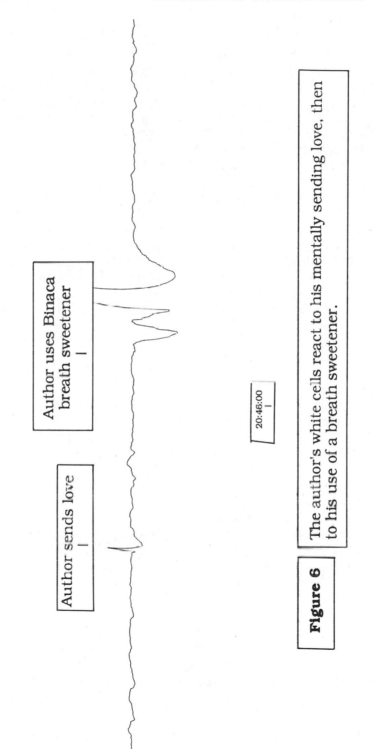

Figure 6 The author's white cells react to his mentally sending love, then to his use of a breath sweetener.

scientists to swallow this concept as reality, but by far the plurality of scientific feet are still dragging.

One philosopher of science, M.B. Hesse wrote decades ago, "Scientific theory in general does not presuppose any particular mode of causal connection between events, but only that it is possible to find laws and hypotheses...which satisfy the criteria of intelligibility, confirmation and falsifiability."

Sheldrake's morphogenetic fields and Backster's primary perception defy that criterion of intelligibility to the feet-dragging scientists still stuck in the mechanistic theory. No other criteria matter to them.

To the mechanistic scientists, one and one equals two and always will. To the scientists with a more spatial Einsteinian point of vantage, one and one might also equal eleven.

Sheldrake is convinced that the unsolved problems of biology remain enigmas because of a restrictive conventional approach and that at least some of the phenomena of life depend on laws or factors as yet unrecognized by the physical sciences. His morphogenetic field theory is daring. It takes Jung's collective unconscious a giant step forward.

One of the original experiments that pre-dated his theory and was carried out by others was training rats to find the right exit from a tank. After they learned the right exit (there was no electric shock), their progeny was put through the same tank exit learning process to see if they learned faster. After 50 generations extending over 20 years, many of the progeny of the trained rats "knew" the right exit without a single shock.

Subsequent experiments in humans have successfully reinforced the idea that the learning process by the few is shared ultimately by the many. Sheldrake sees as a possible explanation the existence of a hierarchy of consciousness which reaches down to the human level and possibly up to a consciousness that created the universe.

Jose Silva also sees a Higher Intelligence at work at different levels, such as universal, galactic, solar systemic, possibly even planetary. He sees the activating of the right hemisphere connecting us to this larger intelligence or consciousness. Certainly, the human abilities that are demonstrated with the right brain activated transcend the accepted boundaries of "intelligibility.' Graduates raise their I.Q., become highly intuitive, and are skilled problem-solvers.

THE SECRET LIFE OF YOUR CELLS BARED

The Silva Method is highly pragmatic. Its aims are to activate more of the mind so that this can become a better world to live in.

The Backster Effect is highly theoretical. Backster does not want to prove anything except that this is a field that deserves serious study by scientists.

The Stone Contention is highly prophetic. If we might use those two words to designate the author's stance, Stone points to a new threshold for developing mental and physical health leading potentially to a higher level of well-being and a longer life.

Once the secret life of your body's cells is bared, the Stone Contention becomes a logical sequitur.

The secret of your body's cells is that they are the loyal subjects of your consciousness.

They perceive your feelings, emotions and attitudes. They react to them.

Although the nature of this reaction must await further research to be fully understood, parallel research points to your consciousness as setting the climate for the well-being of your cells.

Stomach cells are known to react negatively to worry. Ulcers can be the negative result.

The blood's white cells are known to react negatively to stress. Lowered resistance can be the negative result.

Less "known" but seriously suspected reactions add up to 100 percent of all diseases, which might better be spelled "dis-eases."

It is not the Stone Contention that we can control our consciousness perfectly and live forever, but rather that we can eventually be able to die healthy. Even so, the perfect control of consciousness may be generations away, so that what we need to do today is be aware of our consciousness. When it does become involved in the conflicts and stress of this material world, we should know what consciousness steps to take to help compensate for the damage to our cells.

Does this mean treating our cells like our children? In a way – yes. It means being aware of them, lovingly, appreciatively, and considerately.

Your cells have a secret life. They are in love with you.

For your own selfish sake, it behooves you not to let this love go unrequited.

HOW SCIENCE MUST PREPARE TO
HANDLE THE UNBELIEVABLE

The role of science in spelling out the last sentence in scientific terms is important. But don't hold your breath.

Read the last chapter. Put this book down and follow the instructions. And let science catch up to you.

You are the public arena. Usually science, like new laws, is not official until it passes its tests in the public arena. But there is no law that says which must come first.

In this case, the public arena will come first. Science has dictated so. Its accredited academic circles balk at entering the realm of consciousness or the spiritual aspects of the human mind.

So it is up to us – the people who will benefit – to carry the ball. When you read the tested methods spelled out in Chapter 10, reading is good, but doing is better. You are advised to put the book down and enjoy a love affair with your cells.

Meanwhile, the response of science can be accelerated in this public arena, if the public's positive experiences are channeled steadily into health circles via their health providers. Telling your doctor how you relaxed your cells by talking to them and successfully ended certain symptoms may get a "Harrumph," but a number of harrumphs can add up to his personal wonder.

Norman Cousins, editor of the *Saturday Review of Literature*, when diagnosed as having a terminal disease, holed up with laugh tapes, comic books, and other sources of humor, and laughed himself well. He wrote so prolifically about his experiences that it is frequently one of the topics at holistic health conferences. One day, scientists will discover its intelligibility, but meanwhile, as people provide a higher consciousness climate for their cells à la Cousins, the laugh is on the scientists.

The author asked one consciousness researcher just what changes need to take place in the way scientists currently do their research in order for that research to be productive in this new consciousness realm.

Repeatability is the number one bugaboo.

Any scientist reading this statement throws his arms up in despair. It is the end of the road for him. Repeatability is his or her number one guideline.

But should that scientist assume that primary perception exists until its existence is disproved, a new understanding will emerge which will render repeatability less sacred a cow.

That scientist will then understand that his or her thoughts are known by the cells being tested. Therefore when you go over in advance what will be done so as to set up the protocol for repetition, those thoughts are known and they flaw the test. The cells, knowing the protocol, either no longer feel it necessary to react, or, if the protocol is life-threatening enough, they go into a protective "dead faint." Result:

"We have not been able to replicate that effect."

Turn up the equipment's sensitivity ten times the normal and there will still be no measurable electrical activity.

Television shows like "Nova" and "Incredible Sunday" have been faced with this same dilemma because they need to do what comes naturally in such shows: review the procedures for the lighting people, camera men, and other crew members.

Coming up: one straight line on the read-out chart.

WONDER MUST COME BEFORE DISCOVERY

Researchers working in the field of consciousness are bullied. Any who are working on interactions between the mind and the material world are threatened and pressured. More classical scientists frequently contact supervisors to have the consciousness researcher's projects terminated. Students are warned that time spent on such projects will damage their future. And the bullying works. Projects are terminated, jobs are lost, reputations are marred.

The breakthrough must be the building up of wonder. Wonder will permit exploration. Exploration will lead to discovery.

The good news is that wonder is already building up. Institutions are being formed to further research in the consciousness area. The Fetzer Foundation in Kalamazoo, Michigan has consciousness research as one of its main purposes. The Kerr Foundation of Wheaton, Illinois is subsidizing the publication of books on the subject.

An organization has been formed in New York City which acts both as a haven and support group for wonderers. The Reality Club meets twice a month to hear such speakers as Rupert Sheldrake, Fritjof Capra, and Rollo May. These speakers then become members, and the members engage in serious conversations. The club's purpose is: "To arrive at the edge of the world's knowledge, seek out the most complex and sophisticated minds, put them in a room together and have them ask each other the questions they are asking themselves."

Bravo. May their tribe increase.

Centuries ago Giodono Bruno was burned at the stake for daring to suggest that the earth was not the center of the universe. This resistance to new ideas continues in this century, albeit without the stakes. Wilhelm Reich had his papers burned and his laboratory destroyed. He was then put in jail where he succumbed to a heart attack. Velikovsky was "black-balled" by scientists, his publisher boycotted, and advertisements for his books deleted from scientific magazines. What Benveniste is currently experiencing is professional brutality.

The author was impressed by an experiment done in a prestigious hospital several decades ago. It demonstrated the effect of a husband's shock on his wife's body cells and organs miles away. When the author queried the researcher recently for more details to enhance a publication, the researcher denied it was ever performed. Poor memory about yesteryear? Or, concern about today's grant money?

We wonder.

SCIENCE HAS KEEPERS OF THE FAITH

If the philosophers of science are our heroes in the battle to harness consciousness, there are "keepers of the faith" in science who are the villains.

We need to applaud the heroes and hiss the villains.

We need to welcome every effort on the part of the philosophers of science to move the frontiers of scientific investigation beyond the particles of matter and into the energy fields of intelligence and consciousness that are beginning to be detected in the universe.

We need to throw the hot white light of public scrutiny on every action of the "keepers of the faith" intended to intimidate, squelch, brow beat, ridicule and threaten this consciousness research.

A few years ago, Backster was overjoyed when a television network in England expressed a desire to include a sequence on the Backster Effect in one of their science shows. At the request of a prestigious East Coast "keeper of the botanical faith" a botanist from a California university was selected to observe Backster's work during the filming. The botanist was asked to provide a biologist to participate in the sequence.

Backster attached a philodendron to the instrumentation and while on camera the botanist described in detail each of the actions he was about to undertake in an attempt to cause the plant to react. With this elimination of spontaneity and the alerting of the plant cells as to what would happen, of course no reaction took place.

The "keeper of the botanical faith" seemed overjoyed when he examined the chart and saw nary a squiggle in the straight line read-out. But as he made this spontaneous discovery and appeared to feel the elation, there were large reactions from the plant.

Next, it was the recruited biologist's turn to be on camera while the live bacteria in yogurt were being recorded during an attempt to demonstrate how the electroded sample of yogurt would react when a separate beaker of yogurt was fed a nutrient by the visiting biologist. On two separate attempts large chart reactions were demonstrated by the unfed sample when the remote sample was fed by the somewhat impressed guest biologist.

When this dramatic and positive result reached England, other "keepers of the faith" saw to it that this dramatic demonstration was eliminated. The entire yogurt feeding footage was cut out of the show. It could be that there was deemed no room in an established science show for a wavering "keeper of the biological faith," at least if they hoped to sell that show to an American network--which they did.

Reading this is inflammatory enough. But when it happens to a dedicated consciousness researcher, whether his name is Backster or John Doe, who is devoting his life or career to disseminating the "wonder" of primary perception in cells and their capabilities of consciousness, it can be morally devastating.

This is continuing. The "keepers of the faith" will not compromise and certainly not relent. They insist on their own terms and probably always will.

So we turn to the philosophers of science.

NO ROOM FOR NEGOTIATION WHERE
TRUTH IS THE IMPASSE

The author would like to identify philosophers of science and applaud them individually for their heroic work in trying to meet the "keepers of the faith" on their own terms and move them an inch forward. But, to do so would be to target these heroes for the wrath and persecution of their opponents.

Backster feels that the obstructionist tactics used to slow down his progress in biocommunication research need to be identified along with those responsible, to help deter the use of such tactics against future researchers in similar innovative areas. He has kept extensive historical material which should be of interest to the serious philosopher of science and will cooperate fully with university scientists who have a chance to be professionally published and who have demonstrated their philosophical integrity. For this purpose he has provided the address below[2].

Backster does not belittle science. Far from it. But he does belittle scientists who are less than scientists and more the "keepers of the faith."

True scientists keep an open mind. "Keepers of the faith" keep science in closed vaults.

Science needs a new branch.

There is no room for negotiation with scientists who have a closed mind. A new branch of science to cover consciousness research would have to be created and it would need to have new rules of its own. In this way, the "keepers of the faith" could continue to play their own game and peace would be attained as the search moves on unhindered.

The new rules for this consciousness branch of science would recognize first and foremost that the researcher in this area is part of the experiment. The researcher in this area may no longer consider himself or herself as the classical scientist does: an objective observer. There can be no objectivity in the consciousness researcher. That person's consciousness is a part of the experiment. It is one of the variables.

"May I visit your laboratory and observe?" asks a classical scientist.

"I'm sorry," replies the consciousness researcher, "You could interfere with the outcome."

"But all I want to do is observe."

"Can you check your consciousness at the door?"

"Of course not," replies the scientist.

"Sorry, my friend, then it's not possible," insists the consciousness researcher, "Your consciousness will affect the outcome of my experiment."

He wishes he could explain his refusal by citing the time when the late spiritual healer Olga Worrell could not affect the cloud chamber as she had several times the day before because two skeptical scientists had joined the observers. He wishes he could soften his refusal by citing the time the presence of a botanist who roasted the plants after her experiments caused Backster's plants to go into a dead faint, preventing their electrical reaction. He wishes he could enhance understanding of his position by narrating how the Soviet woman named Nelya had to work twice as hard to move an object with the power of her mind when visiting skeptics were present.

But he knows such efforts will be futile. The classical scientist will not accept those examples. The stand-off is non-negotiable.

"Sorry," says the consciousness researcher.

"Slam," says the door.

NEW RULES FOR A NEW SCIENCE

Alan Funt's "Candid Camera" television show was successful for so many years because it was real life. If it was rehearsed instead of spontaneous, goodbye. It would probably get hardly a chuckle, instead of the belly laughs generated by people caught in the act of being themselves.

Your cells perceive when you are acting and when you are being yourself. If you are acting, they will not re-act. If you are being yourself, they are tuned into your consciousness because you are their "god" and they adore you.

A spin-off of the Silva Method attempted to attain recruits by demonstrating at a free public meeting the ability of graduates to describe a person whose name, address, age and sex was provided by a member of the audience, and to detect any illness. It proved to be a dismal failure. Their brain neurons perceived the unreality.

"At ease. It's just a demonstration."

The Backster Effect cannot be demonstrated in a synthetic situation. No primary perception can be measured.

The Stone Contention for better health goes down the drain, too, when the participants go through the motions described in Chapter 10 only because they are curious to see if it works. They get back curious results.

There can be no rehearsed spontaneity.

So, the primary new rule for the new science of consciousness is real life spontaneity.

Another rule is: levels of consciousness need to be recognized. Plants will react to insects being killed. Plants will be sensitive to people. But people will not be sensitive to what is happening to plants or to insects. There seems to be a "pecking order" in levels of consciousness.

Sheldrake recognizes these levels of consciousness. It is like peeling the many layers of an onion. Each level--or species--has a planetary level of consciousness. Eastern religion recognizes these levels, too, using non-scientific terminology, such as "nature spirits," but designating the same thing.

Is there a Higher Intelligence that has as its "layer" the universe itself? If primary perception could some day be subjected to a space test and found to be non-time consuming, non-distance affected, it could well point to such a field of intelligence as the ultimate consciousness in which it functions.

Once we know this and how to contact this level of consciousness, is there anything we can not do to affect the quality of life on this planet?

Sheldrake is in touch with the microcosm of these layers of consciousness and/or intelligence. Each species has its own morphogenetic field. Whereas, Mitchell sees the macrocosm. The work sponsored in part by his Institute of Noetic Sciences has provided laboratory results which only space filled with universal intelligence can explain.

A new rule for the new consciousness branch of science must also be to shrink the no-man's-land between the scientific and the spiritual. Certainly the present frontiers of science need to be extended into areas that have been classically the territory of theologians and philosophers.

The semantics can be separate, but the ideologies need to be open to reconciliation.

Another new rule for the new consciousness branch, is that the "launch pad" needs to be shifted from Newtonian precepts to Einsteinian precepts. Even Einsteinian precepts should be a foundation for study only for as long as that study needs it. As soon as new precepts develop new frontiers of understanding, they become the next "launch pad."

Finally, that idol worshipped by classical scientists called the repeatable experiment must be modified for consciousness research where spontaneity is demanded. Spontaneity produces results. But no two results are exactly the same. Automation is a possible compromise – compromise because it removes the experiment at least partially from real life and genuine spontaneity of consciousness.

Once when Backster provided a lab with automated procedures, they failed to replicate his finding. On investigation, he found that they eliminated the automation.

"We did not have the funds."

Humanity has paid too huge a price for this game that has been played by scientists. Education should take the lead in ending it, but education is a monolithic giant that resists innovation. So it is up to the scientists themselves. Others must break the ties that are binding us to our present dilemma of threatened extinction.

A NEW SCIENTIFIC METHOD FOR CONSCIOUSNESS WORK WILL HELP PROGRESS

Using the automated repeatable experiment today, a small university laboratory may succeed. But then maybe a large university will try and fail. The large university outranks the small university. This pulling of rank goes on and on and succeeds only in neutralizing serious legitimate findings.

In the new scientific method for consciousness research, there needs to be a new respect for meaningful high quality observations even if they do not fit repeatability as a pattern but do fit a predictable or pre-defined category.

For instance, Backster is considering seeking the cooperation of some noted football quarterback. He would like to take a sample of his oral white cells just before a nationally televised game. He would then monitor them in his laboratory during the game. The pre-defined category is a quarterback playing in a nationally televised game. The spontaneity, and non-repeatability, is that quarterback's completion of a pass, or his getting sacked, or his gaining a first down.

Classical scientists can be predicted to run down this particular research on a number of counts. Consciousness researchers, functioning with the new scientific rules adapted for their discipline would find any dove-tailing of playing field action of the donor with mouth cell reaction as serious research.

Well-meaning classical scientists can see a spontaneous

reaction and, because of their protocol training, can refuse to admit what their eyes tell them.

Backster was invited to a laboratory at the University of Southern Illinois to observe a scientist working with worms. In his university lab he was attempting to track down the way these organisms with such simple nervous systems can have such complex actions, thinking, of course, in terms of conventional physiology.

The equipment in that laboratory was the most sophisticated available. An oscilloscope displayed the reactions. These reactions could be jumped onto tape, and could be played back for intensive study. Sensitivity could be increased, chart speed could be varied, and pipette electrodes got the measurements right down to a single cell of the worm.

Not much was happening, though, in the way of reactions.

"Wait a minute," said Backster, "I want to see something." He then walked to the other side of the laboratory where the fresh worm supply was kept in a large beaker. He picked up the beaker and shook it.

There was a dramatic reaction on the oscilloscope which was monitoring that single cell of the worm on the other side of the room.

"Oh, there's got be a loose wire!" cried the researcher, diving under the equipment.

"No wiring problem," explained Backster. "This is the cause-effect phenomenon that I work with all the time."

This is the well-meaning but off-base attitude of researchers in this field. It did not occur to the researcher in this case, that a worm already in a stressed situation caused by the laboratory, could possibly react to additional stress caused by the agitation of his brothers and sisters a few feet away. Only a few hours ago they had all been one big happy family inside a cow's intestines at the slaughter house. Now it was a strange, new, threatening environment.

Backster did not plan to do this. It was done on impulse. It was a spontaneous event.

For the scientist with classical training and a classical viewpoint, what is really happening does not register; primary perception or the possibility of a worm consciousness just does not come across. Instead – a wiring problem! A loose wire makes sense. This other does not.

Suppose this scientist dared to conceive that there was a

connection between Backster shaking the worm supply and the reaction at a distance of the isolated worm, he might well have asked, "Say, Cleve, do you mind going over and repeating that?"

You know the rest of the story. Backster would shake the worm supply again. This time in all probability no reaction. The isolated worm would have adjusted to this particular stress.

What is the classical scientist's reaction to this non-repeatability? It never happened in the first place. Defective wiring. Seismic tremor, maybe. Electrostatic discharge.

He would open a whole new "can of worms." Progress will have hit a stone wall.

Harold Puthoff and Russell Targ who led the Remote Viewing project at SRI for a number of years, are well acquainted with the Backster Effect and would never shout "Wiring defect!"

The same is true of many other consciousness researchers like Ed Mitchell and scores of others with less illustrious names. But nor would they necessarily shout, "Bravo!" Each is sensitive to the rules of the classical game. They try to play by those rules at least outside of the laboratory.

This, too, is a wall impeding their progress, albeit a mite softer than stone.

A COMPUTER ANALOGY

In contrast with the behavioral sciences which have been around since the turn of the century, with the neurosciences which have been recognized for less than two decades, and with cognitive science which has been around for less than a decade, consciousness research has gained its limited recognition only in the past few years.

Each of these probes requires a different research approach. Willis W. Harman, current president of The Institute of Noetic Sciences offers an interesting computer analogy. "Imagine being confronted with a computer for the first time and seeking to understand it," he proposes. "One research approach might be to study the behavior of the device by examining carefully the inputs and outputs." Harman likens that approach to the behavioral science approach to human beings.

On the other hand, another scientist might seek to understand the computer by examining the physical components inside the box, and seeing how the current flows through the circuits and networks. He likens that to the neurosciences approach.

Then there's the scientist who would want to examine the software, analyzing the programs that control the circuits. This is analogous to the study of the human mind in the cognitive science approach.

Still another scientist might want to understand the meaning of the computer's activity, why particular programs are generated--the mind of the programmer.

This is the consciousness researcher's approach.

A well-known British expert in operations research said, "We may be trapped in our own thought-processes."

It is doubtful that any of Harman's four delineated categories will witness many cross-over scientists. Belief systems are effective traps.

But human consciousness is like a flowing river. As old belief systems reach the sea, new freshets at the source are creating a more open stream of consciousness.

A NEW CONSCIOUSNESS IS EMERGING

Call it the "Greening of America" or the "Aquarian Conspiracy," by whatever name a higher consciousness is manifesting in humankind.

It is not being announced by a blare of trumpets or a roll of drums.

It is seeping in quietly and is evident by the average person's increased interest in his or her potential. Whether it be firewalking, spirit channeling, or healing with crystals, it represents a consciousness far more open to what used to be the unbelievable.

It is also seeping in quietly to professional circles.

The author has randomly picked up the program for "Maximizing Human Potential Throughout Life," a professional conference scheduled for January 1989 in Newport Beach, California, and sponsored by the Pre- and Peri-natal Psychology Association of North America. This group is dedicated to the in-depth study of the psychological dimensions of pregnancy and birth and the mental and emotional development of the unborn and newborn child.

The program is studded with standard stuff: birth trauma, humanizing institutional birth, psychological strategies for expectant parents, etc.

But staring out past these old faithfuls are some beacons of the new consciousness: "Cellular Consciousness: The Bodymind Network" presented by Dr. Graham Ferrant whose research has convinced him there is profound imploded wisdom within the substance of the human fertilized egg.   And..."The Practical Applications of Cellular Consciousness in Psychotherapy" also by Dr. Ferrant.

Also in the author's current mail is the announcement of the Second Archaeus Congress to be held that same month in the author's home state on the island of Molokai, let's take a look at it.

The Archaeus Project, headquartered in St. Paul, Minnesota, dares to be at the frontier of consciousness research. It promotes scientific, spiritual, and philosophical communion for those ready to apply new tools to current problems and those of the near future.

The January 1989 meeting announcement lists such presenters and organizers as:

Robert W. Ader, Ph.D., Professor of Psychiatry, Psychology and Medicine at the University of Rochester School of Medicine and Dentistry, speaking on psychoneuroimmunology.

Brenda J. Dunne, Laboratory Manager of the Princeton Engineering Anomalies Research, who researches precognitive remote perception.

Jack Houck, Senior Manager of Advanced Research for McDonnell Douglas Astronautics Corp. who "has conducted extensive practical investigations into mind/matter interactions." He is scheduled for a "Remote Viewing Workshop and Experiment."

Presenters announced in the program include such familiar names as Rupert Sheldrake and Bernie Siegel.

Invitees are being limited to 100 frontier researchers, including Cleve Backster.

This is good news for the reader. It promises a new pragmatism in the study of the secret life of our cells, with the best news of all hidden in one of the objectives of this Congress:

"To examine the concept of cyberphysiology or conscious self-regulation of healing, and its potential application to the problems of the living."

Yesterday – psychoneuroimmunology.

Today – cyberphysiology.

Your mind can control more than your immune system. It can

control your whole body's health.

Maybe the Stone Contention is becoming a fact.

It is heart-warming to note some of the principles recognized at this Second Archaeus Congress. Here are some random concepts:

Often when a patient walks into a consulting room, the surgeon can "know" what his/her self-image is and therefore estimate the patient's ability to survive the operation.

Symptoms of illness are a defense in order that the organism may heal itself. It is illogical simply to treat a symptom.

Exciting things are happening as cyberphysiology is incorporated into allopathic medicine, but there is a long road ahead.

If cyberphysiological principles were practiced on a large scale, it is not inconceivable that the United States could cut its health care costs by $100 billion a year.

It is heart-warming, too, to know that when Cleve Backster was introduced at this Congress, and his work reviewed, he received solid applause from the other scientists.

Footnotes:

[1]William Morrow and Company, inc., New York, 1986

[2]Backster Research Foundation, Inc., 861 Sixth Avenue, San Diego, CA 92101.

Chapter X

How To Affect
The Life Of Your Cells
For Personal Benefits

In Alan Jay Lerner's 1966-67 Broadway play *On A Clear Day You Can See Forever*, the heroine sings to her plants, "Hurry up and grow. It's nice up here!" The plants respond.

Those were pre-Backster Effect days, but a minister named Dr. Franklin Loehr was already praying to plants in that decade and the plants were apparently "hearing" his prayers. In some 700 separate experiments, conducted by 150 persons using over 27,000 seeds and involving 100,000 measurements, prayer made a difference in every case and often as much as 50% additional growth in prayed-for seedlings[1].

Dr. Loehr made it clear that he realized that it was not just plant cells that respond to human thought, but that human cells respond to human thought also, prayerful thought especially.

Being a scientific researcher, Backster usually avoids any speculative comments on the possible applications and pragmatic uses of primary perception; but the author has heard him speak informally on the potential for more holistic approaches to health care – including "talking" to your body's cells. When he participated in the University of Michigan 1973 "Future Worlds" lecture series, his fellow lecturers included Stanley Krippner speaking on "Developments in Parapsychology in U.S. and Russia;" U.S. Supreme Court Justice William O. Douglas talking on "The Future of Our Political System;" R. Buckminster Fuller, "Designing a Future World;" and Arthur C. Clarke, "Life in the Year 2001." So Backster was able to stretch a bit and talk about "Communication in the Biotic World."

In this chapter, the author stretches a bit, too. But this is years later than the early 70s and a time when progress has accelerated on a hyperbolic curve to a dizzying speed.

Millions of people have already started talking to their bodies' cells and seeing beneficial results. They have also talked to the cells in the bodies of their loved ones and seen the same positive results. In this chapter we tell you how. It is the Backster Effect and the Silva Method in action.

It is the new medical term: cyberphysiology.

UNDERSTANDING ENERGETIC CAUSES BEHIND MATERIAL EFFECTS

Split the atom and you get energy. The matter of this physical universe is polarized energy. Energy is the cause of matter. Matter is the effect.

Science has defined its scope as the material realm. To delve into the causal realm is not scientific. This is rather the realm of the religionists and philosophers.

Consciousness is creative. It is energy. It is in the creative or causal realm. It is currently not possible to be totally scientific in working with consciousness, like the Backster Effect, or spiritual healing, or subjective communication or "talking" to your body's cells.

Still, the religions and philosophies of the world – at home in this realm – have long proclaimed the powers of human consciousness which such current phenomena as the Backster Effect, Remote Viewing, and the Silva Method of Mind Control demonstrate.

The Rosicrucians, who were behind the single eye of our dollar bill and whose secrets and symbols have been studied for centuries, believe that there are planes of consciousness which extend into the particles of matter. They see the presence of consciousness in plants, and therefore intelligence, manifesting in plants' nutrition, nervous systems and even thought processes. The Rosicrucians carried this belief into the study of nature in action with corroborating evidence in a thousand directions, starting from the intelligent movements of the zoospores of seaweed and including the purposeful movement of the anthe- roza of ferns and mosses. The Rosicrucians' *Secret Doctrine* pro- claims that there is manifested consciousness on all planes of life and being.

The theosophists also have a *Secret Doctrine*. Authored by one of the movement's founders Madame Blavatsky over a century ago, it too proclaims levels and degrees of consciousness perme- ating all space, and all matter. It exploded into the thinking of her day with repercussions still echoing and making their impact on the so-called New Thought religions.

The Unity Church is an example of New Thought harnessing Higher Intelligence. Centered in Lee's Summit, Missouri, it has on-going absent healing work from coast to coast.

HOW TO SET THE STAGE FOR
MIND/BODY COMMUNICATION

Scientifically, from what we know today, the success of the procedures to communicate with physical body cells can only be attributed to these levels of consciousness permeating all space. The primary perception of your liver cells – that is, their ability to perceive your loving care and support – can be explained only by these fields of consciousness. Even if they could not be explained at all, the effects are there and can add years to your life.

The most important part of this book to the reader is this final chapter. Why then is it not the first instead of the last?

The reason is: Nine chapters have been devoted to preparing you for success. That success is based on your belief. If your beliefs are as classical as the classical scientists, like them you will be far less likely to succeed. If, on the other hand, the first nine chapters of this book have encouraged you to accept the possibility that there is more going on in this universe than meets the eye, and that consciousness has something to do with it, get ready for some "miracles."

By reading this book and learning what consciousness re- searchers like Backster are able to record, you have set the climate for success in your own personal ability to affect the cells of your body with your thoughts.

You have been doing this right along, but only in a negative way. You felt anger at somebody, the need for revenge, seething hostility. You were jealous, insecure, fearsome. You felt impatience, frustration, and despair.

All of these feelings are stress. Stress is a killer. You have been killing your body's cells. Eventually, you will kill yourself.

You will not be alone. We all do.

The trick is to recognize stress and substitute something else for it, something the opposite of stress. It will then cause the reverse effect. The opposite of death is life.

But our mind is like a computer. We are programmed to think and behave the way we do. So we need to change the programming. How do we do that?

HOW TO CHANGE THE POLARITY OF YOUR THINKING FROM LIFE SAPPING TO LIFE GIVING

Programming your mind is so simple, it should be taught in kindergarten. It is an easy two steps.

But it will probably be a long time before it is taught at any level of our educational system because it breaks two basic educational rules.

The two simple steps are relax and daydream.

Class requirements are just the opposite: sit up and pay attention.

You better make up your mind right now that you will take matters into your own hands – in school or out – if you want to talk your cells into helping you lead a healthier life.

Once you are able to relax thoroughly, then mental picturing, as you do when you daydream, is programming.

The reason this is so is that relaxation slows your brain waves so that their frequency is smack in the middle of their 1-20 usual range. Relax physically and mentally and you slow your brain wave frequency to about 10 pulsations per second. That is where programming becomes possible.

Also, the right hemisphere of the brain – usually at a much lower level of activity than the left hemisphere – increases its activity to more balance the thinking.

Balanced thinking is physical world logic and non-physical world creativeness. The right hemisphere could be our connection to the fields of consciousness that are currently being hypothesized. The reason for saying this is that when we activate the right hemisphere – that is, when we relax and mentally picture – we can communicate outside of the ordinary channels.

If you want to change your thinking from life sapping to life giving, you need to program your mental computer accordingly.

HOW TO PROGRAM YOUR MENTAL COMPUTER

The use of meditation in the treatment of heart disease is currently being investigated. One leading researcher has been Herbert Benson, M.D. associate professor of medicine at Harvard Medical School. He found that meditation causes what he calls the "relaxation response," the reverse of the typical "flight or fight" stress response. He found that alpha waves increase in intensity and frequency in meditation.

Relaxation used in meditation is the first step of the two-step formula. The second step is visualization, as we do in relaxed daydreaming.

Dr. Dean Ornish handles this well. He also has been on the faculty of Harvard Medical School and with the Massachusetts General Hospital in Boston. In his book "Stress, Diet and Your Heart,"[2] he instructs the reader, "Keeping your eyes closed, imagine that your heart is beating strongly and regularly. With each beat, picture that heart pumping efficiently and effortlessly."

When you do that are you talking to your heart cells? You most certainly are. It is the beginning of cyberphysiology.

But the researcher who in the author's opinion has done the most to bring this procedure into planetary use is Jose Silva, founder of the Silva Mind Control Method, and with whose work the author has been intimately associated for over a decade. There are now over eight million in the world who have taken the four-day training and are able to "talk" to their own cells in a healing way but also transcend space and do the same with the cells of other people.

Many of the steps about to be delineated for you in this chapter are adapted from the Silva Method. Further details on this Method can be obtained from two books by Jose Silva with the author.[3]

Enough is given here now to provide the reader with more than he or she really needs to contact body cells. After all, even the person who plops into a comfortable living room chair after a hard day at the office and begins to worry about lost sales, negative cash flow, or diminished profits is engaging in cell talk.

Relaxed daydreams about stressful situations are stressful messages to the cells of the heart, lungs, liver and other vital organs. These stressful messages stress the cells, adding to the load of stress already carried from that stressful day. Being creative, these negative daydreams perpetuate these problems.

Relaxed daydreams about solutions instead of problems create what you want – solutions, not problems. And they send positive, creative messages to the cells of the vital organs, giving them a chance to recuperate from stress.

Mental pictures tend to create what they picture. You will not usually see movies on a plane that depict air crashes – not since a flight film showed a plane where the landing gear jammed and the plane showing that film then experienced that same problem. Three hundred relaxed minds picturing can create that picture.

You can worry yourself poor and sick or daydream yourself wealthy and healthy. You can program yourself out of the negative way of habitually thinking into the positive way.

PROGRAMMING FOR A CHANGE
IN SPECIFIC THINKING

Any programming requires relaxation. This relaxation should be both physical and mental – and in that order.

It is best to adopt a sitting position in your favorite chair where you will not be disturbed and to continue to use that chair for your programming sessions until it becomes so natural with you that you can do it anywhere, anytime.

There are many ways to relax. The author will list some below – physical first. Pick the ones that seem the most natural for you to do (at least three) then do these three in the order listed.

When you complete these three methods of relaxing physically, then relax mentally. The way to relax mentally is to visualize some tranquil scene. There will be a list of those.

Next, give yourself a positive statement about your thinking, "ordering" it to change from negative to positive.

Finally, end your session. Do so by counting from one to ten, stopping a couple of times along the way to remind yourself that when "I open my eyes at the count of ten, I will be wide awake feeling great."

We will review these steps later, but meanwhile follow these steps for physical relaxation: First, sit in a comfortable chair, then close your eyes and do three of the following:

A. Take a deep breath and as you exhale, relax your body.

B. Count backwards from 20 to 1 or from 10 to 1.

C. Feel yourself getting heavier in the chair with every backwards count or with every normal breath you take.

D. Be aware of every part of your body and relax it: scalp, forehead, eyes, face, neck shoulders, etc.--all the way to your ankles and toes.

E. Pretend you are descending in an elevator, perhaps in a department store or in a coal mine. Feel yourself getting into a deeper and deeper state of relaxation with each lower floor.

Once you are relaxed physically, here are some typical natural scenes to choose from in order to relax mentally. Pick a scene that you are most familiar with as being a passive scene for you, or, use a scene from your past experience where you remember how serene it made you.

A passive scene that will help you to relax mentally might be:

A babbling brook	A tree "house"
A quiet stretch of beach	A meadow
A lake-side spot	A mountain scene
A backyard rocking chair	A hill-top
An outdoor swing	A porch chair

After you relax physically, imagine you are really at such a tranquil spot. Do so just for a minute or two. You are then relaxed physically and mentally. You are ready to program.

Here are some ways to program yourself out of negative thinking into positive thinking. This changes the message you are sending to your cells from: "Life is ending" to "Life is just beginning." Pick two ways from the following with which you are the most comfortable – one verbal and one visual, in that order.

Verbal programming (repeat mentally to yourself from one to three times each session):

* Negative thoughts do not influence me. I reject them. Positive thoughts bring me all the benefits I desire.

* I am courageous and confident. Every day in every way I get better and better. I let go of the past and set goals for the future. I reach them.

* I understand the fallacy of negative thinking. It no longer

interests me. I also understand the power of positive thinking. It interests me strongly. From now on I think positively.

* I no longer put my creative energy into problems. Instead, I visualize solutions. I no longer think about how little I have. Instead, I think of my blessings and my rosy future.

Visual Programming (adopt one picture and "see" it for a few seconds after you complete the vocal programming):

* See yourself a millionaire.
* See yourself carried on the shoulders of your admiring colleagues.
* See yourself radiating charm, efficiency and creativeness.
* See yourself getting a meritorious citation.

Reviewing, these are the steps for programming yourself out of health-sapping pessimism into health-producing optimism.

1. Sit in a favorite comfortable chair and close your eyes.
2. Do the steps to relax physically.
3. Be in the tranquil place you have selected for a minute or two.
4. Repeat the verbal programming statement you have selected – three times.
3. See yourself in the picture you have adopted from the suggested list. Hold the picture as if it was real for five or ten seconds.
6. End your programming session by counting from one to ten mentally, reminding yourself that when you open your eyes at the count of ten you will feel wide awake and great.

Reread these instructions. Make your choices. Commit the verbal statement to memory. Find a comfortable chair, put the book down. Close your eyes and do it.

HOW TO "TALK" TO YOUR CELLS

When you relax and picture another person, your brain neurons are in touch with their brain neurons. It is as if you are not as separated from this person as the physical world would have you believe, that somewhere, you are together.

Jung called this "place" the collective unconscious. Sheldrake calls it the morphogenetic field. Peter Russell calls it the global brain. Jose Silva calls it Higher Intelligence. Whatever you call the route it takes, your brain neuron to brain neuron call never results in a wrong number.

But it can result in a disconnect.

To avoid a disconnect, you must follow two rules. You must talk in a loving, equal way. You must talk in a mutually beneficial way.

The same is true of your own cells. You must talk in a loving way. You must communicate benefits to themselves and to you if they accept your instructions.

Dr. Carl Simonton's approach as an oncologist to his cancer patients – which had much to do with the onset of psychoneuroimmunology – was to relax, go inside their body mentally, and visualize the immune system's white blood cells martialing their forces and routing the cancer cells.

Josc Silva's approach is also to relax decply, but thcn to put yourself in an imaginary laboratory and fix yourself up. This you could also do for another person.

We will start with the Simonton approach because it does not entail as much methodology, and then we will go to the Silva Method.

Some years ago, at a radio manufacturing company in the mid-west, executives decided to change the tint of fluorescent lighting to see the results. When they made the light more of a pinker shade in one assembly room, production when up ten percent. When they made the light more of a blue shade in another assembly room, the same thing happened; production went up ten percent. They decided to put back the original fluorescent lighting. Production went up another ten percent in both rooms.

What the workers were responding to was the fact that somebody cared. You respond also to people caring. Your cells respond to your caring.

This is an elaboration of what was referred to in Chapter V.

It is so easy to contact your body's cells right now and tell them that you care, and their response is so positive, you should read the instructions, put the book down, and do it.

You relax physically and mentally as before.

You take a trip through your body, thanking your organs and cells for a job well done.

You count to ten and end your session.

All you need is an understanding of what "take a trip through your body" means. You can do this any way you wish, but here is a typical trip:

You imagine you are sliding down a hair on your head to below the scalp. You thank your hair for being your crowning glory and ask those hairs to send your word of thanks to the rest of the hair on your body. Do the same with the scalp, sending the appreciation to all of your skin cells. Descend to the skull and do the same, thanking all the bone matter in your body. Next the brain. It deserves your thanks, being the best computer yet in existence. Thank your eyes, ears, nose, mouth for those senses. A tip of your hat to the stomach – what a chemical plant that is. And so on to your intestinal tract for absorbing nutrients, your colon for that thankless waste-removal job, ditto your kidneys. Don't overlook the reproductive system while in that part of the body. Take a ride back in a blood vessel, thanking the red and white corpuscles, the plasma, the vessels themselves, returning via the heart. ("Thank you, you magnificent pumping station") and also stopping off at the lungs ("You do good work.") Exit finally by shimmying up a hair at the same point you started.

Remember the movie *Fantastic Voyage*? Take one.

THE SIMONTON METHOD OF GIRDING THE IMMUNE SYSTEM TO GREATER EFFECTIVENESS

Dr. Carl Simonton adapted the Silva Method while oncologist at Travis Air Force Base in California. He taught his cancer patients to relax, pretend they were able to go inside their body, and then to picture their white blood cells attacking their cancer cells and eliminating them from the body.

He found that it did not matter that the patient's visual image of this process was not scientifically correct. The concept, however pictured, would get the message across and there was a decided positive effect. Cancer was being cured at Travis Air Force Base with a greater success ratio and in less time.

Reviewing the Simonton Method, the steps are:

1. Relax physically and mentally.
2. Imagine you are inside your body where the cancer is located.
3. Mentally picture the white blood cells in the blood vessels and capillaries there.
4. Program with mental pictures, talk to them in a friendly way with mental words. Encourage them to eject from the body, the cancer cells already dead and dying as a result of the radiation or chemical therapy.
5. See yourself perfect and end your session.

The better you are at relaxation, the better your communication to your body cells is received.

There is a tendency on the part of the average person to seek assistance through music or voice cassette tapes in relaxing.

The ads for these music tapes are quite convincing. Here is one: "Easy flowing piano melodies make you feel like you are reflecting in front of your fire place."

Another titillates you with: "Harp, flute and vocal tones guide you on a peaceful journey back in time and space."

Then the promoters of voice tapes offer you: "Recharge yourself with refreshing energy. A subtle voice whispers words of encouragement." Or, "Tune your body and mind to bright alertness with a surge of energy."

Many of these tapes are well put together. But they are tapes. They are electro-magnetic representations of the real thing. There is no consciousness involved.

Your body cells do not respond to synthesized communication. They respond to your consciousness as it mentally vocalizes a message to them, or mentally visualizes the way you – their lord and master – wishes them to be.

A tape is like the classical scientist's repeated experiment. It does not work with cell consciousness. Your spontaneous act to contact your body cells with your conscious desire is the language they understand.

It is real life. Give them real life and they give real life back to you.

HOW TO BE IN TWO PLACES AT THE SAME TIME

Consciousness is a marvel to behold. You can send your consciousness to your kidney cells and beseech them lovingly to get rid of certain poisons in your body, and still know what's going on around you. Yes, your consciousness can be in two places at the same time and maybe even more.

In 1940, the *New Yorker* magazine contained a cartoon by Charles Addams that neatly depicted an enigma of the quantum theory in physics. It showed a skier speeding down a snowy hillside leaving twin tracks behind him. These tracks separate and pass a huge pine tree, rejoining to continue their parallel path on the other side.

Could the skier be on both sides of the tree at the same time?

Yes, says the quantum theory and convincing evidence exists for this enigmatic behavior.

In 1974, Helmut Rauch, an Austrian physicist, fired neutrons one at a time through a silicon device so that the flight path split into two branches about an inch apart, then rejoined about three inches later. A detector registered that each neutron traveled down both branches simultaneously. An inch on the neutron scale of distance is much larger than the diverging paths of that cartooned skier.

Incidentally, neutrons make up about half our body's weight.

Classical scientists who are still thinking Newtonian thoughts find it easy to say something is impossible.

Consciousness scientists who are working in the Einsteinian and quantum modes find it difficult to say something is impossible.

The Silva Method is a case in point.

HOW TO USE THE SILVA METHOD TO HELP YOUR-SELF AND OTHERS TO BETTER HEALTH

It is impossible to give the reader the Silva Method 4-day training in a page or two, but it is possible to obtain that training through the books already mentioned which your author wrote in collaboration with the founder of the training, Jose Silva.

Better yet, take the training.   Silva Mind Control is listed in most major city phone directories. If you were a graduate, here is how you would heal yourself.

1. You would go to your alpha level instantly with just three deep breaths, visualizing in a certain way.

2. You would count backwards from 10 to 1 to go to a deeper level, known as the laboratory level.

3. You would greet a male and a female counselor that awaits you in this laboratory which is the creation   of your own imagination.

4. You would visualize yourself in front of a screen in that laboratory.

5. You would focus your intelligence on the problem area, and what steps might be taken to correct the problem.

6. If you ask one of your counselors to help, ideas will come.

7.   Using whatever tools, equipment, or medications were needed, you would then fix yourself up.

8.   You would then see yourself perfect – no sign of the

problem.

9. You would then thank your counselors and end your session in the prescribed manner.

It is best to help yourself as soon as possible after a health problem arises. Serious problems should get this attention from you three times a day, spending five to 15 minutes each time.

You can put other people in front of your laboratory screen, fix them up, and get positive feedback from them, as your consciousness transcends space limitations in the creative realm, and you "talk" your friend's body cells well.

It is interesting to note that as Jose Silva began this training in 1966, Backster was discovering primary perception, one of its principles, that very same year.

BACKSTER'S GOALS FOR THE FUTURE

As Backster's retirement age approaches, he hopes to retire from polygraph work but not from consciousness research. His primary perception work has opened a door. But now, this door has led to ten other doors.

He sees cryogenics – the freezing of cells – as one of these doors that need to be explored. That technology will be useful in overcoming the present time limit of about eight hours imposed by the life of the cells when removed from the donor. The cells' reaction to the donor's thoughts and/or emotions could then be measured from the other side of the earth, and days after removal.

Backster has hesitated to use living cells or tissues from a donor's body, other than white cells. Even spermatozoa are dangerous for him to use from a political viewpoint. With so many scientists ready to "do a trip on him," why give them that opening.

Tissues require controlled temperature and other environmental conditions which Backster is not currently equipped to adequately provide. But there is another deterrent. It will first be necessary to be certain that conditions be avoided in handling in vitro tissue that might create a communication reversal to the detriment of the donor. White cells are always exposed to emergency situations, and always doing battle in vivo. Therefore in vitro there is minimum risk of their feeding back negativity to affect the well-being of the donor.

We are all constantly affecting our body cells negatively and causing their earlier demise by our stressful thoughts. We do not need to repeat that crime in the laboratory.

Whether or not there is attenuation of primary perception with distance remains a critical factor in its understanding.

Reduction of the signal over large distances would make classical scientists heave a sigh of relief. It would then brand primary perception as another wave type phenomenon, probably with some location on the electro-magnetic frequency scale.

On the other hand, if primary perception is not affected by large distances and takes no time to occur, then like the quantum theory, it is in two places at the same time.

This would present Einsteinian scientists with a field day, and it would shove pioneers on the frontiers of consciousness over the line into the very one-ness of the universe. They would be faced with the omnipotence, omniscience, and omnipresence of a continuum of consciousness that permeates all space.

The rest of us would be divided into two camps: God forbid. And God be praised.

LOGISTICS FOR A SPACE EXPERIMENT

If primary perception is not time-consuming and does not attenuate with distance, it would be an enlightening discovery that would affect all humankind. Space is a necessity to determine this. Halfway around the earth is not a sufficient distance as it would require only a fraction of a second. Biological reaction alone can take a second or so, making such determination on earth impossible. An unmanned space shot would require a complicated package.

As a manned space experiment it would be simple. It would take no equipment in the space vehicle, no time allotment from the astronauts.

You would not have to put a package of cells in space which would require controlled conditions to incubate them and then monitor them in space as a donor on earth experiences stress. Turn it around. Periodically actuate a batch of the astronaut's white cells from cryogenetic storage in San Diego as he or she spontaneously undergoes the stress of a space flight.

The planned Mars probe would be perfect as the time lapse for wave-type communication, or light itself for example would be at least 15 minutes, depending upon the Earth-Mars separation at that time.

Backster is hopeful about getting cooperation from NASA on the next manned space venture. There is a possible operational advantage to NASA in knowing of any stressful occurrence minutes before they hear about it vocally on the radio from the astronauts.

Backster is hopeful also about acquiring some new equipment.

He is anxious to upgrade his video equipment, the nucleus of his monitoring. He needs to free himself of the read-out charts and have these read-outs jump right onto a track on the video tape. The technology to do so is available. He would also like to go portable with some of his equipment to expand opportunities.

A better microscope video camera would enable him to see the migration of in vitro cells. Oral white cells move through capillaries and across body fluids to reach the scene of an infection. How do they know? He is equipped to see the purposeful movement of mouth white cells now with a time lapse video recorder, but a microscope video camera and monitor with higher resolution would enable him to better observe and attempt to influence cell locomotion. This would help decide whether the present exploration of chemical signals is really a dead-end street and that direct perception by the cells is really the answer.

Cyberphysiology could then really come of age. Physicians may teach us what to "say" to which cells in order to accomplish a cure.

INSIGHTS CAN BE HAD INTO EVOLUTION

Backster is a scientist primarily, and a theorist only reluctantly. He realizes that good data can be thrown out with bad theory.

The author has been stimulated into re-examining the theory of evolution in his conversations with Backster. Some interesting ideas have emerged.

Horizontal evolution seems to be a natural situation. The fit survive. Refinements occur in species to help survival. But vertical evolution – a new species springs from an old species – is harder to swallow if your consciousness is aware of the existence of higher consciousness.

The author would love to ask Backster, if he had been the judge in the famous so-called monkey trial, would he be on the side of the evolutionists or religionists? He would be on the spot. He would have to respond religionist, despite his lack of belief in any one religion but rather in a spiritual understanding of the universe.

Any word that recognizes a higher intelligence behind the emergence of life forms is bound to be more appetizing to researchers into the Backster Effect.

It would be of value to have Backster, perhaps later in his life and research, to let go and express himself freely on what his observations of primary perception in its many forms has brought to him in the way of an understanding of life and the universe.

Meanwhile, he owes a great deal to the world's use of the polygraph; to the help of such people as Robert E. Henson, his partner and administrator of the Backster School of Lie Detection for more than two decades, and Mary Ann Henson, office manager and executive secretary of Backster Associates; to the research collaboration of Steve White; and to the dedicated support of several philosophers of science. It all gives him the chance to continue his research. He does not hope to convert the classical scientists. He is realistic about that.

"The best one can hope to accomplish in a lifetime," he says, "Is to make them a little less sure of themselves."

A CONVERSATION WITH CLEVE BACKSTER

One fall day in Backster's San Diego laboratory, Sam the cat was dozing on top of a television monitoring set; the tortoise was sleeping for the seventh day in a row, head protected under a ledge; and the fish were swimming slowly back and forth the length of the huge glass wall tanks.

Backster brought two cups of coffee over to the table and sat down opposite the author. It seemed an appropriate time to subject him to the interrogation he was once skilled at doing when with the CIA.

STONE: Can we talk to our body's cells?

BACKSTER: Before steroids, body builders were sending "grow" messages to their muscles, mentally seeing them develop. and they responded dramatically.

STONE: Can we do more than that today?

BACKSTER: We realize today what negative thinking does to our body's cells. Sure, they get the message. The wrong message. We interfere with their normal functioning. We make ourselves sick.

STONE: Would it work the other way around?

BACKSTER: Of course. (He sipped his coffee.) But we had

better stop the negativity first. We are affecting other people, too. When our heart cells suffer from our thoughts or state of mind, other people's heart cells could be affected also. I see it in this lab all the time. A donor's cells react to the donor's emotions. The donor leaves. The donor's cells can then react to my emotions.

STONE: Brain neurons, too?

BACKSTER: Yes, as you well know. Mental healing communication is fine, but I'm not sure we're ready to tap other people's thoughts yet. We all have a bit of growing to do before we can handle it. As we grow, it will become more within our grasp. What we are doing in this lab is moving us in that direction.

STONE: There is a growing awareness of laughter being an effective form of therapy. Is this a form of cell communication?

BACKSTER: Real laughter is. Not forced laughter. The mind set is what does the communicating, not the guffaws. Laughter communicates joy of living to body cells. If you were a body cell wouldn't that make you feel better?

STONE: "Talking" to our body cells, subjective communication, primary perception – it's all so natural. Why is it looked on as supernatural?

BACKSTER: Humans may be here on earth to learn to cope with the material world. Until this lesson is learned, the physical senses are dominant and these other abilities are perhaps relegated to a back seat. We may be in the process of graduating now.

End of conversation, as we both sat sipping our coffee in silence.

WHAT THE FUTURE MIGHT HOLD FOR MIND-TO-BODY CELL COMMUNICATIONS

The occult life of your body cells, thanks to Backster et al, has been de-occulted. The cell is not a closed unit of your body, automatically doing its job. It is doing its job, but not automatically. You have a measure of control. It is like a climate control, with your mental attitudes creating the shifting climes in which that cell grows and has its being. Your cell does not have to look at the window to see if it is raining. Your negative thoughts are perceived instantly. These thoughts sap your cell's vital energy. Your positive thoughts are perceived instantly. They charge your cell with vital energy.

That's the simple truth. The discovery of the psychosomatic

causes to illness was the initial recognition of that truth. Psychoneuroimmunology took that recognition a practical step forward. Now cyberphysiology takes it all the way.

Our thoughts, feelings, and attitudes are known by our cells. This mental activity can cause their demise or cause their well-being. We make ourselves sick. We can make ourselves well.

That is only the beginning.

A man relaxes, pictures his superior at work, explains in a brotherly way why his idea, if adopted, would be an advantage to all. The next morning, he is called into his superior's office. The suggestion is being adopted.

This, too, now happening on an increasing scale, is only the beginning.

Subjective communication, brain cell to brain cell, can also take place on a diplomatic level, solving international problems practically overnight, that would otherwise linger, fester, and maybe boil over into conflict.

If this is beginning to happen, the author is not aware of it, but that it will happen soon, the author is convinced.

Will it also become possible to send one's consciousness out to consciousness looking for a body, and influence not only the sex of a fertilized egg, but the intelligence, personality, and evolvement of the consciousness that is about to make it its home?

Will it become possible to communicate with consciousness wherever it is in the universe and share wisdom?

Humankind is emerging from a Newtonian cocoon into a new awareness of who it really is.

Stay tuned.

Footnotes:

[1] *The Power of Prayer on Plants*, The New American Library, New York, NY, 1969

[2] Holt, Rinehart and Winston, 383 Madison Avenue, New York, NY 10017, 1982

[3] *You the Healer*, H.S. Kramer, Tiburon, California, 1989. The Silva Mind Control Method for Business Managers, Pocket Books, New York, NY 10020, 1986